adorable animals
you can paint

Jane Maday

NORTH LIGHT BOOKS
Cincinnati, OH
www.artistsnetwork.com

Published by North Light Books, an imprint of F+W Publications, Inc., 4700 E. Galbraith Rd., Cincinnati, Ohio 45236. (800) 289-0963. First edition.

Other fine North Light Books are available from your local bookstore or art supply store, or direct from the publisher.

10 09 08 07 06   6 5 4 3 2

Distributed in Canada by Fraser Direct
100 Armstrong Avenue
Georgetown, ON, Canada L7G 5S4
Tel: (905) 877-4411

Distributed in the U.K. and Europe by David & Charles
Brunel House, Newton Abbot, Devon, TQ12 4PU, England
Tel: (+44) 1626 323200, Fax: (+44) 1626 323319
Email: mail@davidandcharles.co.uk

Distributed in Australia by Capricorn Link
P.O. Box 704, S. Windsor NSW, 2756 Australia
Tel: (02) 4577-3555

Library of Congress Cataloging-in-Publication Data

Maday, Jane.
    Adorable animals you can paint / Jane Maday.
            p. cm.
    Includes index.
    ISBN-13: 978-1-58180-738-7 (pbk. : alk. paper)
    ISBN-10: 1-58180-738-4 (pbk. : alk. paper)
    1. Painting—Technique. 2. Animals in art. 3. Decorative painting. I. Title.
    ND1473.M33 2005
    751.45'432—dc22
                                        2005014474

Development Editors: Kathy Kipp and Chris Read
Content Editor: Jolie Lamping Roth
Production Coordinator: Kristen Heller
Cover Designer: Clare Finney
Interior Designer and Layout Artist: Dan Phillips
Photographer: Christine Polomsky

metric conversion chart		
To convert	**to**	**multiply by**
Inches	Centimeters	2.54
Centimeters	Inches	0.4
Feet	Centimeters	30.5
Centimeters	Feet	0.03
Yards	Meters	0.9
Meters	Yards	1.1
Sq. Inches	Sq. Centimeters	6.45
Sq. Centimeters	Sq. Inches	0.16
Sq. Feet	Sq. Meters	0.09
Sq. Meters	Sq. Feet	10.8
Sq. Yards	Sq. Meters	0.8
Sq. Meters	Sq. Yards	1.2
Pounds	Kilograms	0.45
Kilograms	Pounds	2.2
Ounces	Grams	28.3
Grams	Ounces	0.035

about the author

Born in England and raised in the United States, Jane Maday has been a professional artist since she was fourteen years old. At sixteen, she was hired as a scientific illustrator for the University of Florida. After college, she was recruited by Hallmark Cards as a greeting card illustrator, and worked there for a happy eight years until her children were born.

Jane now lives in scenic Colorado with her husband and two children and a menagerie of animals. In addition to writing art instruction books and articles, Jane licenses her work onto numerous products, such as cards, puzzles, stitchery kits, T-shirts, etc.

acknowledgments

This book would not have been possible without the help of many talented and gracious people. When painting realistic animals, it is important for an artist to have good reference materials, and I would like to thank Sharon Eide and Elizabeth Flynn for their wonderful photos of kittens and puppies and Dave Maslowski for his brilliant images of birds and wildlife. The gang at Digigraphics helped me so much by teaching me to take my own photos for many of the step-by-steps in this book and did a skilled job with the developing and finishing process.

Thanks must also go to the amazing staff at North Light Books, especially editors Kathy Kipp and Chris Read. You made a slightly intimidating project into one that was a complete joy. Your support and guidance were invaluable.

A final thank you must go to my husband, John, and our children, Ian and Margaret. You shared my enthusiasm, gave me confidence when I felt insecure, and understood all those times when my mind had a hard time coming back to Earth from the "art planet."

dedication

This book is dedicated to my mother, Jean McCoy, for your unfailing love and support, no matter where my life's journey has taken me. If I can be half as good a mother to my children as you were to me, I will feel that I've done a good job!

table of contents

introduction

I have always wanted to be an artist, and my journey to this point in my life has been a long and joyous one, although there have been pitfalls along the way! When I first began painting, I found it frustrating when I couldn't duplicate a teacher's example of a technique or image. I want to take this time to remind you that this book is meant only to guide you on your own path. If your paintings don't look exactly like mine, that's fine because the painting that you make is yours. I have tried to make this book as helpful as possible in showing you how to take different elements from my work to help "jump-start" your own. The most important thing I can teach you is not how to hold a brush or mix a color, although those things are necessary to know. What I want to share most of all is that painting should be a process full of joy. Try to relax and have fun, because what you feel in your heart comes through onto the paper. Welcome to my world, my new friends!

Some Notes on Painting

In this book I have used Golden Fluid acrylics and Winsor & Newton watercolors. I like the color clarity in these brands. Whatever brand you choose, try to pick professional grade paints over the student grade if you possibly can. Professional grade paints have more pigment in relation to the binder, so you get cleaner, brighter, richer colors. Choosing low quality paints is a false economy, because you end up needing more paint in order to achieve strong color. It is also frustrating to struggle with an inferior product as well as your own inexperience!

Most brands will have the same color names as I have specified in the forthcoming projects. An exception will be the word "quinacridone" as in "Quinacridone Crimson." If using another brand of paint, substitute "Alizarin Crimson." While many brands have the same color names, the colors themselves may vary. An excellent example of this is Payne's Gray. I prefer Payne's Gray to be a dark indigo; some brands are noticeably less blue.

Some Tips on Mixing Colors

You will notice that some colors are stronger than others. When mixing, always mix a small amount of the stronger color (red, for example) into the weaker one (such as yellow). If you mix weak into strong, you'll end up using a lot more paint until you find the right color mix.

When using watercolors, it is perfectly acceptable to re-wet the dry paints on your palette. There is no need to set out fresh paints for each painting session. For acrylics, invest in a palette made especially for keeping acrylics moist (such as Sta-Wet by Masterson), and be sure to spritz the paints with water and seal the lid tightly when you are finished working.

A Final Note

Your health is important, and for that reason, try to choose paints that are nontoxic. Some paints, such as the Cadmium and Cobalt colors, contain heavy metals. For that reason I always specify the hue of that color. The word "hue" after the color name, such as "Cadmium Red Medium Hue," indicates that it's a nontoxic form of that color. However, you should still use good painting habits and never eat or drink while you are painting. Wash your hands frequently, and never put your brush in your mouth to moisten it or to reshape the point.

Good luck and happy painting!

part one: getting started

materials & techniques

I always recommend buying the best quality materials you can afford. Buying cheap supplies is actually a false economy because they need replacing more frequently. Also, isn't it hard enough battling your own inexperience; why should you have to fight with inferior products too?

Paints

For this book, I have used both Winsor & Newton watercolors, and Golden Fluid acrylic paints. Both these brands have a high pigment to binder ratio, so you get bright, clean colors. They also have a smooth, creamy consistency. I work with the paint quite thin, so I prefer the fluid acrylics packaged in a little bottle over the thicker acrylics in a tube. I dilute the paint with water, but you can use a medium such as a gel retarder if you wish.

Brushes

Different types of brushes vary greatly, as you will discover. Many of the techniques in this book require control, and a delicate point on the brush is important. My favorite brushes are made by Silver Brush, especially the Ultra Mini Designer Round series. These brushes have an amazingly fine point, even on the larger sizes. A larger brush holds more paint, so you load it less frequently than a tiny brush. If you use a different brand, you will need to purchase smaller sizes to achieve the delicate details. For painting fur, I believe that a grass comb brush is essential! This type of brush has bristles that separate at the end, so you can paint several hairs at once. Once you try it, you will wonder how you ever got by without it.

Palettes

For watercolors, I use an enamel butcher's tray. I like having a large surface for mixing and diluting the paint. For acrylics, a palette that keeps the paint moist is important, or you will find yourself getting frustrated by the quick drying time. I use the Sta-Wet Palette by Masterson. The sponge underneath keeps the paint from drying. You can make a substitute using your butcher tray by wetting a pad made of folded, high-quality paper towels. Place a sheet of acrylic palette paper (Masterson or Winsor & Newton) that has been soaked in hot water over the top. Apply your paints to this surface, and spray them periodically with water from a spritzer bottle.

Palettes

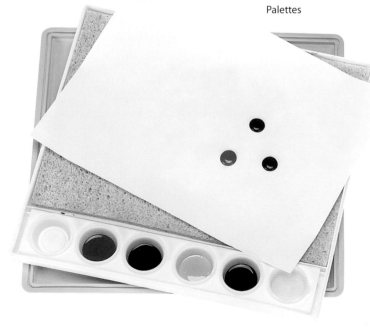

Masking film

All the projects in this book use clear masking film instead of masking fluid. I buy the Frisket brand in rolls, but it is also sold in sheets. You'll find it in the airbrush section of craft and art supply stores. To use the masking film, you will also need a sharp craft knife, such as a no. 11 blade X-Acto knife. Put a new blade in at the start of each painting. Your blade must be sharp enough that you can cut through the masking film without pressing down on the blade. Don't be intimidated by this product that you may have never used before! Once you get the hang of it, you'll find it much easier than masking fluid.

Paper

The type of paper I use is specified at the beginning of each project. It is worth noting here, however, that in order for the masking film to work properly, you must have a fairly smooth surface to your paper. I recommend Canson Montval cold-press watercolor paper (do not use rough surface paper), illustration board or Strathmore 500 series bristol board. Make sure you ask for the 500 series, as it takes paint better than the other types of bristol board, which are meant for drawing.

Other supplies

At the beginning of each project, I have listed all the supplies you will need. A few indispensable products are: graphite transfer paper, drafting tape (not masking tape), tracing paper (for copying the patterns in this book), and a sharp pencil with a fairly hard lead, such as 4H. In some projects I use items such as a sea sponge (for stamping texture), pastel pencils and cotton swabs.

Before painting, try to set up a comfortable area for yourself with good lighting and ventilation, so everything is working in your favor. You'll need a water container to rinse your brushes, and some nice, thick paper towels for blotting your brush. Remember not to eat or drink while you work, and wash your hands frequently if you tend to get paint all over yourself like I do! Are you ready? Then let the fun begin!

Basic techniques

In the next section, I will be describing some basic techniques that will help you complete the projects in this book. It's a good idea to read this section before going further, as I address in detail methods that are used for each project, including preparing the paper, using masking film, and some basic and specialized brushstrokes.

Brushes

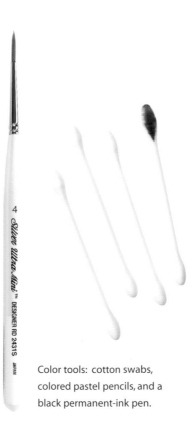

Color tools: cotton swabs, colored pastel pencils, and a black permanent-ink pen.

7

pre-painting techniques

Transferring the Pattern

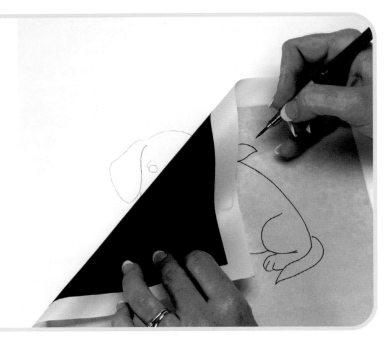

All the paintings in this book come with patterns that you can trace and transfer to your paper. I use the same method for transferring each time. Transfer paper can be purchased in several colors, as well as plain graphite.

Use drafting tape to tape the pattern to the paper, because drafting tape will not mar the surface of the paper. Use a mechanical pencil with a very sharp, hard lead (or a stylus) to transfer the pattern.

Pull back the pattern and transfer paper to make sure the pattern has transferred onto the paper.

Mounting the Paper to Prevent Buckling

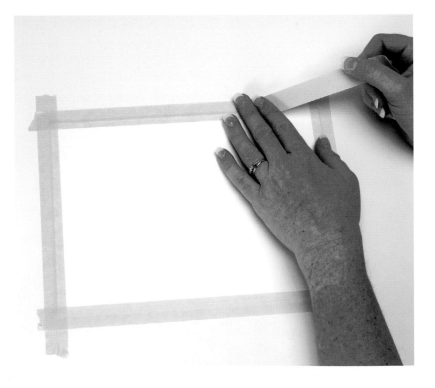

I prefer to paint on cold-press watercolor paper or 500 series Strathmore bristol board. This method of mounting the paper works for both types of paper. (The 500 series bristol board accepts paint better than other series and is the only type I would recommend.)

I prefer using watercolor paper in a block (a pad that is gummed on all four sides.) If you use single sheets of paper, you should mount them to a board to prevent buckling when the paper gets wet. Use drafting tape, rather than masking tape, because it can be removed without damaging the paper. Choose a backing board slightly larger than your paper.

Tape it securely on all four sides, so all the edges are covered. If the paper does buckle, wait until the project is completely dry. Then remove the paper from the backing board. Flip it over and tape it to the backing board again with the image side facing down. Lightly mist the paper with a water spritzer. As the paper dries, it should dry flat. Your project should always be completely dry before removing it from the backing board.

Using Masking Film

Masking film is a transparent sheet of plastic that has a mild adhesive on one side, much like Contact paper. I like to use masking film rather than masking fluid because I find it easier to get controlled, precise coverage, and I can remove a small section at a time, which is impossible with masking fluid. I think you will find that working on each section individually is less intimidating than being faced with an entire painting at once.

1 Cut the sheet of masking film to the approximate size needed for the project. Peel the masking film off the backing. To avoid having the masking film stick together, pull away the backing from the corner and start applying it to your paper from the corner, gradually releasing it from the back sheet and pressing it to your drawing as you go. Handle the masking film as you would handle Contact paper.

2 Smooth out any bubbles that appear, working from the center outward to push the air bubbles to the edge.

3 At the beginning of each new project, make sure to put a new blade in your cutting tool. It is important that the blade is sharp enough to cut through the masking film layer without putting much pressure on the knife. Cut around the outline of the drawing. Be careful not to press too hard. You want to cut the masking film without cutting the paper beneath it.

4 Start at the corner and peel off the excess masking film to expose the background. You may need to guide it with your fingers so that the drawing stays covered. If your drawing is especially intricate, remove the background masking film a small area at a time. Now you are ready to paint.

Using Tape to Mask

In a pinch, it's possible to use transparent tape as a substitute for masking film. This method works best if you have just a small area to cover; I don't recommend it for large, complicated areas. It is a bit more finicky to use because it peels off in small strips, but some people may find it more comfortable to use a product they have around the house.

1 This technique works best on small projects. Pull off strips of Scotch Magic transparent tape (this type of tape pulls off more easily than other kinds of tape) and place over the area that needs to be covered. Make sure to slightly overlap the edges of the tape strips so paint doesn't seep into the cracks.

2 Use a sharp craft knife to cut around the image, then peel away the excess tape in the same manner as if you were using masking film (see page 9). Peel away the excess tape in small strips instead of one whole piece. Paint as usual. Make sure the paint is completely dry before removing the last taped area.

Tip

It is best not to leave tape on the paper for an extended period, as it will adhere more strongly over time. If you have trouble removing the tape, heat it with a hair dryer to make the tape easier to lift. The same is true with masking film and masking fluid.

painting techniques

Using a Wet Palette

If you are unfamiliar with acrylics, you may be frustrated by the speed with which they dry on a palette. This problem can be solved by using a wet palette, which can easily be purchased at craft and art supply stores.

A wet palette keeps your acrylics from drying up as you work. The palette is provided with a sponge that you soak before placing it on the palette. Do not wring out the sponge after wetting it.

Next, take the disposable palette paper that comes with it and run it under hot water until it's translucent. Place it on top of the sponge and use that as your palette surface. These palettes also come with an air-tight lid that will keep your paints moist for several days.

Loading the Brush

"Loading the brush" refers to filling your brush with paint. The method is the same for both acrylics and watercolors.

1. When you pull your brush out of the water, gently run the brush tip across a paper towel so it's not dripping wet. Place a small amount of paint onto the palette. Wet the brush and use the brush with water at the edge of the paint dollop to create a small puddle.

2. Twirl the brush through the paint to create a point at the end of the brush, so it retains its fine point. Before painting, run the brush tip lightly across a paper towel to remove any excess paint.

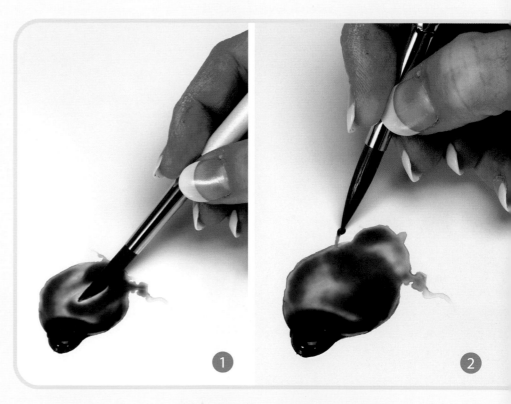

Painting a Background Wash

A "wash" of paint means to cover an area with a thin, watery layer of paint. I prefer to use water rather than mediums when painting with acrylic, so this method works for both watercolor and acrylic paint.

Wet the paper with clean water on the brush. Load your brush with the desired paint color and blot the excess on a paper towel. For a vignette background, do not start painting at the edge of the paper. Start painting just inside the wet area, so the paint bleeds softly out to the edges. For a flat background, start at the edge and gradually work your way down the page, using back and forth strokes.

Glazing Over a Shadowed Area

"Glazing" refers to painting a transparent color on top of a color that is already dry. Make sure the first layer of paint is completely dry, or any subsequent layers will "lift" the paint underneath. Use a delicate touch with the brush; do not scrub. Glazing can add depth to your colors that is hard to achieve otherwise.

To glaze, make sure your paint is very transparent; thin the paint with water. Paint a glaze over the area where you want to add just a tint of color.

Stippling

"Stippling" means to paint with a series of little dots. In this book, I use the stippling technique to paint a lamb's fleece.

Use any worn-out bristle brush or a brush specifically used for stippling. A dry blending brush is shown in this photo. Load the brush by patting the tip up and down in the paint. Test the brush tip on a paper towel to make sure there is no excess paint. Hold the brush vertically and pat the paint onto the paper.

Shading

If you want a subject you are painting to have a three-dimensional form, it will be necessary to add some shading. This means to add shadows to the part of the subject that is facing away from the light source in the painting.

I like to add shading with transparent washes. Using opaque paint to create shadows will make your subject look flat, rather than rounded. The color of your subject should glow through the shading. The placement of a shaded area depends on the direction of the light source in the painting, so a shaded area should always appear on the other side of the subject to the highlight.

Lifting Out Color

When using watercolors, it is possible to create light areas by "lifting" some of the color. Traditional watercolorists do not like to add white paint to their pictures, and, while I am not a purist in this regard, I do like the glowing effects that this technique can achieve. This technique only works with watercolors. To attempt it with acrylic paint, you must work quickly and lift the paint before it dries, rather than after.

1 Make sure the paint is completely dry before lifting out color. Put plain water on the brush and paint the element with the water. Do not scrub the paper with your brush.

2 Take a paper towel or tissue to lift the color off the paper.

Using Acrylics Like Watercolors

When I paint with acrylics, I like to paint in a watercolor manner most of the time. This gives the finished painting a smooth surface with colors that have depth, because I can glaze over them.

I use the fluid acrylics that come in bottles because they are thinner than the paint that comes in tubes. Squeeze a blob of color onto the wet palette. Wet the brush with clean water and mix the water into the paint to further thin it. Before painting, test on a piece of scrap paper. You should be able to apply the paint in a transparent manner.

Using a Cotton Swab

Occasionally I like to add some soft pastel pigment using a cotton swab as a brush. This can give a softer look when adding a little warmth to the inside of an ear or to a little pink belly. This is an optional technique, but I thought you might like to give it a try.

1 Rub the cotton swab over the tip of the pastel pencil to pick up the pigment.

2 Rub the pigment on the tip of the swab onto the paper. This creates a softer smudge of color as compared to using paint.

Painting Fur

As this book is about painting animals, it is important to practice making fur strokes before you tackle any of the projects.

After loading the filbert grass comb brush, check to make sure the paint is not so thick that the bristles are stuck together. Test on a piece of scrap paper before painting on your project. The strokes on the left are too thick and too straight. The strokes on the right are fluid and tapered, which is the best way to create fur. Remember that your strokes should always follow the direction of fur growth. In several of the mini demos, the directions state that you paint "opaque fur strokes." This refers to the paint being opaque rather than transparent and thin.

For more on painting fur, see "Creating a Fur Map" and "Painting Fur and Feathers Step by Step" on pages 16-17.

creating a fur map

For many of the projects in this book, you will notice I recommend that your brushstrokes follow the direction of fur growth. Beginners may find it helpful to create what is called a "fur map" to help visualize the way to move the brush.

Below, I have included a photograph of an adorable Westie from my files. I often attend dog shows to take reference photos. That way I am sure of getting pictures of the best examples of the breeds. To prepare for painting, lay a sheet of acetate or tracing paper over your photograph. Trace the outline of the animal; this is what you will transfer down to your painting surface. To create a fur map, study your photo carefully. Imagine you are stroking the animal with your hand or grooming its coat. You always move your hand in the direction of fur growth, don't you? Otherwise you would muss the animal's fur and could cause discomfort. Draw arrows on your sketch of the animal to help you remember the direction to stroke with your brush. In the illustration, this is indicated by the colored arrows on the Westie sketch. You do not need to transfer the arrows to your painting; just keep looking at them for reference.

To create fur strokes with your paint brush, begin at the hair root. Gently increase pressure through the middle of the stroke and lift the brush gradually at the end, so the line of paint gradually tapers. You may want to practice a flicking motion for fur that is wavy. Remember, the hairs are not straight lines; they conform to the animal's body.

The step-by-step guide on the next page will provide some tips to help you create realistic animals. You may want to practice these before you tackle some of the more complicated projects in the book.

Reference Photo

Sketch Showing Fur Direction

painting fur and feathers step-by-step

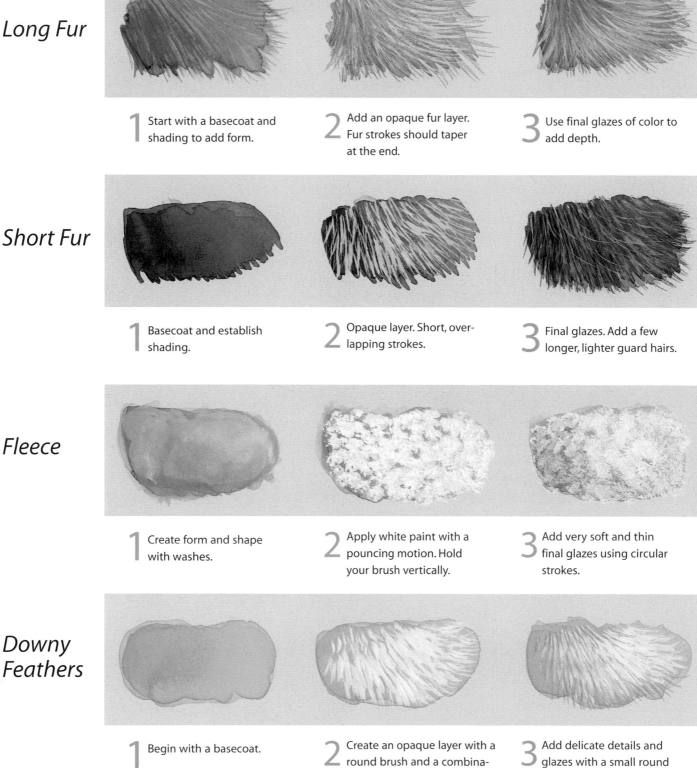

Long Fur

1 Start with a basecoat and shading to add form.

2 Add an opaque fur layer. Fur strokes should taper at the end.

3 Use final glazes of color to add depth.

Short Fur

1 Basecoat and establish shading.

2 Opaque layer. Short, overlapping strokes.

3 Final glazes. Add a few longer, lighter guard hairs.

Fleece

1 Create form and shape with washes.

2 Apply white paint with a pouncing motion. Hold your brush vertically.

3 Add very soft and thin final glazes using circular strokes.

Downy Feathers

1 Begin with a basecoat.

2 Create an opaque layer with a round brush and a combination of thick and thin strokes.

3 Add delicate details and glazes with a small round brush.

part two: demonstrations

subject & complete-scene demos

This section consists of two kinds of demo: the mini-demonstration and the complete demonstration.

Mini-Demonstrations

These demonstrations focus on the main subject without the distractions of backgrounds or settings. I have gone into greater detail than in the main projects at the end of this section, so you may wish to refer back to these mini-demonstrations if you feel you need greater explanation for a look or technique. I have also included some more detailed explanations for some background elements, such as flowers, berries, stone, and wood. Patterns for the mini-demos can be found at the back of the book on pages 124-125.

Baby Bird (page 19):

We'll start with watercolor techniques. I have chosen to paint a baby bird first because there is very little detail to the feathers. Some of the details are quite delicate, so make sure you have a brush with a fine point!

Wren (page 20):

Now that we have painted a baby bird, we can take a step up and paint an adult bird. In this demo, we will practice with more glazes.

Lamb (page 21):

This demo gives you a chance to practice the stippling technique featured in the lamb and kitten project later in this book. Painting fleece can be a bit easier than fur, because the brushstrokes can be less precise, and there is less detail.

Fawn (page 22):

This is the first attempt at fur strokes. A fawn's fur is quite smooth, so it is a good place to start. These techniques could also be applied to paintings of foals or calves. Don't forget the knobby knees!

Bunny (page 23):

Watercolor fur is painted in a more transparent manner than acrylic, and this bunny demo gives you a chance to try it on a fairly simple form.

Long-Haired White Cat (page 24):

Painting long hair takes more confidence than short hair, because your brushstrokes should be smooth and flowing. White fur can also present a challenge because it is easy to make it look dirty. In this demo, less is more!

Beagle Puppy (page 26):

When painting baby animals, the expression is very important. This demo gives you a chance to practice achieving an appealing look. And who can resist a puppy's little round tummy?

White Terrier (page 28):

So far we have practiced long fur and short fur. The difference here is that long hair on a dog is generally a little coarser than on a cat.

Ginger-Striped Kitten (page 30):

It is more difficult to capture the charm of a kitten's face than the grace of an adult cat. Try to keep the fur soft and the eyes appealing.

Berries (page 32):

I absolutely love painting berries! Putting a touch of nature into your paintings is a great way to add interest to your composition, and the placement and color can help lead the viewer's eye through the picture to the focal point.

Flowers (page 34):

Many of the projects in this book feature flowers, as they are an excellent way to add color and charm to a painting. I have painted them in watercolor here, but the same techniques can be applied with acrylics thinned with water.

Stone and Wood (page 35):

This demo features some simple techniques for creating believable backgrounds and natural textures. You can use these techniques to paint stone walls or pathways, or old wooden fences and barn walls.

Complete Demonstrations

At the end of this section, there are ten full painting demonstrations with complete materials lists and extensive step-by-step instruction for each aspect of the painting. Traceable patterns are included with each demonstration.

baby bird

Color Palette

Winsor & Newton Artists' Water Colours: Winsor Blue (Green Shade), Raw Umber, Burnt Umber, Yellow Ochre, Raw Sienna, Sepia, Payne's Gray, Burnt Sienna, Titanium White.

1 Transfer the design onto the paper. Apply the masking film and cut around the baby bird. Remove the excess film to expose the background. Wet the background with clean water and the 3/4-inch (19mm) flat brush. Apply a wash of Winsor Blue (Green Shade) with the no. 12 round brush and let it bleed softly out into the wet paper. Let dry. Paint the twig with a wash of Raw Umber. Let dry, then detail with Burnt Umber.

Remove the masking film from the bird. Begin by painting the beak with Yellow Ochre and the eye with Burnt Umber. Next, give the breast a wash of Raw Umber and Raw Sienna mix, starting at the edges and letting it fade toward the middle. Finally, paint the wings, head and tail with a transparent Raw Umber and Burnt Umber mix. When all is dry, indicate the feet with Burnt Umber.

2 Add form and shape with Sepia on the no. 4 round brush. Again, use the Sepia on the no. 4 round to add loose, downy feathers to the top of the wings. Use Payne's Gray to add a pupil. Shade the belly with Burnt Umber.

3 Glaze the wings, tail and head with Burnt Umber on the no. 4 round. Slightly darken the stripe on top of the eye with Sepia. Add a Sepia glaze under the wings and on the bottom of the belly. Smooth any hard edges with plain water on the brush. Add a glaze of Yellow Ochre over the wings, belly and head to add warmth.

4 Paint the tip of the beak with Burnt Sienna on the no. 4 round. Add a Titanium White highlight to the eye and the beak. Paint a few delicate feather strokes to the cheeks, above the eye and overlapping the wings with Titanium White. Finish detailing the beak with Sepia.

wren

Color Palette

Winsor & Newton Artists' Water Colours: Winsor Blue (Green Shade), Raw Umber, Sepia, Yellow Ochre, Burnt Umber, Burnt Sienna, Payne's Gray, Titanium White.

1 Transfer the pattern onto the paper. Apply the masking film and cut around the bird to expose the background. Wet the background with the 3/4-inch (19mm) flat and clean water. Apply a wash with the Winsor Blue (Green Shade) and the no. 12 round, letting it blend softly out to the edges. Let dry. Paint the branch with Raw Umber. Let dry. Detail with Sepia and a glaze of Yellow Ochre. Remove the masking film.

Where the belly meets the wing, paint a wash of Raw Umber that gradually fades as it travels up to the breast. Paint another Raw Umber wash where the head meets the breast. The eye and legs are Burnt Umber. When the breast is dry, mix Burnt Umber and Burnt Sienna and paint a wash on the wing, tail and facial stripes. Finally, add a touch of Sepia to the beak.

2 With the no. 4 round brush, paint a pupil with Payne's Gray. Outline the eye with Sepia. Use Sepia to build form on the head and wing with the no. 4 round. Use the 1/8-inch (3mm) filbert grass comb and Sepia to add form to the belly. Add a glaze of Burnt Umber to the belly. Paint a few strokes of Raw Umber to the golden area at the top of the breast. Add another glaze of Burnt Umber to the wing and tail, if the color appears too pale.

3 Use the no. 4 round and Yellow Ochre, with a little bit of Burnt Umber along the bottom, to glaze the beak. Moisten the brush with clear water and wipe out the light areas on the wing and tail. Let dry. Add details with Sepia. Create a gray color with a mix of Payne's Gray and Sepia, then glaze shadows onto the cheek, neck and breast.

4 With Sepia on the no. 4 round, add details to the legs and feet. Add highlights to the eye and the legs with Titanium White. Use Titanium White to create white wing spots and a few delicate white feathers over the wing and down the breast. Add final details to the wings and head with Burnt Umber, mixed with a touch of Sepia.

lamb

Color Palette

Golden Fluid Acrylics: Raw Sienna, Cadmium Red Medium Hue, Raw Umber, Burnt Umber Light, Payne's Gray.

Liquitex Acrylic Artist Colors: Titanium White.

1 Trace the pattern onto the paper. Cover with masking film, cutting out and revealing the background area. Wet the background with clean water and the 3/4-inch (19mm) flat. While still wet, lay in the ground with Raw Sienna, and the background behind the lamb with a Cadmium Red Medium Hue and Raw Sienna mix, letting them blend together. Before the background is completely dry, paint loose straw with Raw Umber and Burnt Umber Light on the chisel edge of the flat brush. Let dry.

Remove the masking film from the lamb. Paint the shadow areas on the lamb with transparent Raw Umber. Move your brush in little circles as you paint to help create the fleecy look. The white areas are plain white paper. The eye is Burnt Umber Light and the nose, the inside of the ear and the hoof receive a glaze of a Raw Sienna and Cadmium Red Medium Hue mix.

2 With the no. 12 round, glaze the shaded areas of the lamb with Raw Sienna. Let dry. Start building texture into the fleece with Raw Umber. Do not put texture into the light areas. Add form around the eye, mouth and nose with delicate Raw Umber strokes.

3 Paint the pupil of the eye with a Payne's Gray and Raw Umber mix. Outline the eye with the same mix. Let dry. Add a Titanium White highlight and lashes overlapping the eye.

4 Load the no. 5 dry blending brush with Titanium White and stipple on some white fleece over the textured area. To stipple, hold the brush as close to vertical as you can, moving it in a controlled pouncing motion. With the no. 12 round, add a final glaze with a Raw Sienna/Raw Umber mix over the shadow areas. Add final shading to the hoof with a slightly darker mix of Raw Sienna and Raw Umber. Add some extra darkness to the straw under the lamb with Raw Umber. Add a touch of the Cadmium Red Medium Hue and Raw Sienna mix around the eye. Let dry. Go back and touch up any of the fleece if the shadows get too dark.

fawn

Color Palette

Golden Fluid Acrylics: Burnt Umber Light, Raw Sienna, Raw Umber, Burnt Sienna, Payne's Gray, Cadmium Red Medium Hue.

Liquitex Acrylic Artist Colors: Sap Green Permanent, Titanium White.

1 Transfer the drawing to the paper. Place masking film over the entire area and cut away around the fawn to reveal the background. Wet the background with clean water and a 3/4-inch (19mm) flat brush. Apply a wash of Sap Green Permanent. While still wet, apply a wash of Burnt Umber Light along the bottom. With the edge of the flat brush, loosely pull out some Sap Green Permanent grass. Let the background dry.

Remove the masking film from the fawn. Paint the fawn with a wash of Raw Sienna; leave unpainted white paper for the white areas. Darken the top of the head and the back with a wash of Raw Sienna. The eyes are Burnt Umber Light, and the nose and hooves are Raw Umber.

2 With the no. 12 round, paint a wash of Burnt Sienna across the back and head to develop shadows and form. Let dry completely. Glaze with Raw Umber to add more shadow and to form the body. Paint the pupil and around the eye and nose with a black made of a mix of Payne's Gray and Burnt Umber Light. Paint the mouth with Raw Umber. Let dry. Mix Cadmium Red Medium Hue with Raw Sienna, then glaze the inside of the ears. Let dry.

3 Use the 1/8-inch (3mm) filbert grass comb and a mixture of equal parts Titanium White and Raw Sienna to paint the opaque fur layer. In the white fur areas, use Titanium White to paint the opaque fur layer. Let dry. Rim the ears with delicate strokes of Burnt Umber Light.

4 Glaze the fawn's fur with the no. 12 round and a mix of Raw Sienna and Burnt Sienna thinned with water. Glaze the shadow areas with Burnt Umber Light. Add Titanium White highlights to the eyes and nose. Make a mix of Raw Umber and Payne's Gray and, using the no. 4 round, add eyelashes to the eye area and detail the hooves. Use the 1/8-inch (3mm) filbert grass comb and a touch of Raw Sienna mixed with white to add the spots.

bunny

Color Palette

Winsor & Newton Artists' Water Colours: Olive Green, Hooker's Green, Raw Umber, Burnt Umber, Raw Sienna, Permanent Rose, Payne's Gray, Sepia, Titanium White, Yellow Ochre, Winsor Red, Permanent Sap Green.

1 Transfer the design onto the paper. Apply the masking film and cut around the bunny to expose the background. Wet the background with clean water, using the 3/4-inch (19mm) flat. Apply a wash of Olive Green, and before it dries, apply a wash of Hooker's Green to the ground area, making vague grass shapes with the chisel edge of the brush. Add more Hooker's Green under the bunny to create a shadow.

Basecoat the bunny's head with Raw Umber on the no. 12 round. Begin at the ears and work toward the nose, letting the paint fade toward the muzzle. The white areas of the bunny are plain paper. Let the head dry before you paint the body in the same manner. The eye is Burnt Umber and the inside of the ear is a pale wash of Raw Sienna mixed with a little Permanent Rose.

2 Using the no. 12 round, paint the pupil of the eye with Payne's Gray. Outline and shade the eye with Sepia, then soften the outline with Burnt Umber. Shade the bunny with transparent Sepia washes, blending with clean water. Let dry, then glaze some more shading with Burnt Umber. Add a Titanium White highlight to the eye, and wipe out a secondary highlight with clean water and the no. 4 round brush.

3 Use the 1/4-inch (6mm) filbert grass comb with Burnt Umber mixed with a touch of Sepia to paint fur strokes. The first strokes on the face are shorter than the first strokes on the body. Paint little opaque hairs with a mix of Titanium White and a touch of Yellow Ochre. Use the no. 12 round to add a warm touch to the ear with a mix of Winsor Red and Yellow Ochre.

4 Finish the inside of the ear with a little more Burnt Umber shading. Glaze the fur with the no. 12 round and a mix of Burnt Umber and Raw Umber. When you glaze, make sure to use a light hand so you don't smear the painting underneath. Use a very sharp pencil to add whiskers. Finally, add some blades of grass with the no. 4 round and Permanent Sap Green mixed with just a touch of Winsor Red. To make the blades overlap the bunny, lift them out first with clean water, then go back and paint them with the green mix. Indicate some blades of grass by painting the negative spaces between them.

long-haired white cat

Color Palette

Golden Fluid Acrylics: Payne's Gray, Raw Sienna, Cadmium Red Medium Hue, Burnt Umber Light, Burnt Sienna.
Liquitex Acrylic Artist Colors: Sap Green Permanent, Titanium White.

1 Transfer the drawing to your paper. Apply the masking film and cut around the cat. Lift excess film to expose the background. Wet the background with clean water and a 3/4-inch (19mm) flat brush. Paint the background with Payne's Gray. While this is still wet, apply more Payne's Gray underneath the cat for a cast shadow. Let dry. Remove the masking film from the cat.

Paint the cat's eyes with a mix of Sap Green Permanent and a little Raw Sienna. Paint the inside of the ears and the nose with a mix of Cadmium Red Medium Hue and Raw Sienna thinned with water. Paint the forms and shapes with a transparent wash of Raw Sienna on a no. 12 round. Leave the white areas untouched.

2 Begin shading the cat by outlining the eyes with a mix of Burnt Umber Light and Payne's Gray on a no. 12 round (or smaller brush if you prefer). Add the pupil with this same mix. Add more water to this mix and shade in the eyes around the pupil and under the top lid. All of the shading, in this step, on the white cat's body is done with the same transparent wash of Burnt Umber and Payne's Gray on a no. 12 round. Paint the shape of the mouth, shade between the eyes, shade inside the ears and establish the shape of the ruff. Shade the back of the neck and along the top of the back. Then shade along the haunch and back leg to separate it from the body. Shade the front leg and underneath the tail.

Tip

Leave plain white paper for the lightest fur. Where light shines on white fur, you don't see any detail so you don't need fur strokes.

3 To begin the long fur layer, load a 1/4-inch (6mm) filbert grass comb with Titanium White. Make long sweeping strokes of the brush, lifting at the end so the hair tapers. Follow the direction of hair growth and paint the fur following the shape of the cat's body and limbs. Avoid painting the very lightest areas of the fur where the light is strongest—that area is the white paper. Extend the fur outward into the background color. Add fur to the rim of the ears, pulling the strokes upward. Glaze the inside of the ears and underneath the nose with Burnt Sienna.

4 Paint the details, starting with the highlight in the eyes, using Titanium White on a no. 4 round. Pull a few fine hairs over the eyes and inside the ears. Highlight the nose on the left side. Glaze a little Raw Sienna into the eyes and let dry. Thin the Titanium White with water and add a secondary highlight in the eyes under the pupils.

Load a no. 12 round with Raw Sienna and a touch of Burnt Umber and make delicate strokes in all of the shaded areas to help define the individual hairs and to warm up the shaded areas a little. If some of your shaded areas get too dark, go back in with Titanium White and re-establish some of the lighter fur.

With very transparent Payne's Gray, glaze over the deepest shadowed areas along the top of the head, between the ears, along the haunch, behind the front leg, and along the tail where it curves.

beagle puppy

Color Palette

Golden Fluid Acrylics: Raw Sienna, Burnt Umber Light, Raw Umber, Carbon Black, Payne's Gray, Cadmium Red Medium Hue, Burnt Sienna.
Liquitex Acrylic Artist Colors: Titanium White.

1 Transfer the design onto the paper. Apply the masking film and cut around the drawing to expose the background. Wet the background with clean water using the 3/4-inch (19mm) flat brush. Apply a wash of Raw Sienna, and while it's still wet add some Burnt Umber Light under the dog as a shadow. Let dry. Remove the masking film from the dog, except for the bandanna area. Paint the puppy's eyes with Burnt Umber Light and the nose with Raw Umber. Paint the light brown areas on the face with Raw Sienna. The dark brown fur is given a basecoat of Raw Umber. The white fur is plain white paper. Always stroke in the direction of fur growth.

2 Use the no. 4 round and Carbon Black to paint the pupils of the eye and the dark areas of the nose. Use the no. 12 round and a mix of Payne's Gray and Raw Umber to paint a transparent wash for shadows in the white fur areas and to darken shadows in the brown fur areas. With the same brush and mix, outline the eyes. Use Burnt Umber Light to add shading to the light brown fur areas.

3 Highlight the eyes and nose with the no. 4 round and Titanium White. Add a secondary highlight to the eyes with a glaze of Titanium White. Create the opaque fur layer for the dark fur with a mix of Titanium White and Carbon Black on the 1/4-inch (6mm) filbert grass comb. Remove the masking film from the bandanna and basecoat with a mix of Cadmium Red Medium Hue and Burnt Sienna. Use the no. 12 round and a mix of Raw Umber and Cadmium Red Medium Hue to paint shadows on the bandanna. Paint the opaque fur layer on the light brown fur area with a mix of Raw Sienna and Titanium White. Use Titanium White to paint the opaque fur where the white fur overlaps another fur area. Add a few more touches of Burnt Umber Light to the face.

4 Use the no. 4 round and Titanium White to paint the print on the bandanna. With the same brush and thinned Titanium White, glaze some highlights on the bandanna. With the no. 4 round and Carbon Black, refine the dark areas of the fur. Since a beagle's fur is smooth, paint with long, smooth strokes. Use the no. 4 round to add highlights to the black fur, with a mix of Titanium White, Payne's Gray and Carbon Black. Use the same mix to refine the shadows in the white fur. Use Titanium White with a touch of Raw Sienna to add highlights to the brown fur. Take a cotton swab and a warm red pastel pencil and rub the swab onto the pencil to pick up some soft color. Use the swab to rub the soft color on the puppy's belly and place a small bit under the nose.

Tip

To achieve the soft pinks on a puppy's belly and under its nose, use a cotton swab to apply the pigment from a red pastel pencil. See page 15 for more details.

white terrier

Color Palette

Golden Fluid Acrylics: Raw Sienna, Burnt Sienna, Burnt Umber Light, Raw Umber, Cadmium Red Medium Hue, Payne's Gray.

Liquitex Acrylic Artist Colors: Titanium White.

1 Transfer the drawing to the paper. Place masking film over the area and cut around the terrier to reveal the background. Wet the background with clean water and a 3/4-inch (19mm) flat brush. Apply a wash of Raw Sienna, and while this is still wet, place some Burnt Sienna around the dog. Let dry and then remove the masking film.

With a no. 12 round, paint the eyes with Burnt Umber Light, the nose and inside of the mouth with Raw Umber, the tongue and inside the ears with a mix of Raw Sienna and Cadmium Red Medium Hue (ratio of 3:1). Then use thin washes of Raw Sienna to begin indicating form. The white areas are clean, untouched paper. Let dry, then add some thinned Payne's Gray to indicate shaded areas around the face, chest, legs, haunch and tail. Paint the collar with Payne's Gray.

2 Outline the eyes and add the pupil with a mix of Burnt Umber and Payne's Gray (ratio of 2:1) to make a soft black. Use this same mix to shade the nose and add the nostrils. With thinned Burnt Umber Light, shade the top and edges of the tongue and shade inside the ears and around the eyes. Using a no. 4 round, start adding form around the nose and mouth with short delicate strokes of thinned Burnt Umber. Continue adding form to the darkest shadowed areas, such as along the side of the head, where the ears meet the top of the head and around the feet.

3 Using a 1/4-inch (6mm) filbert grass comb, mix a tiny amount of Raw Sienna into Titanium White to warm it. Begin adding fur all over the dog using long strokes and following the direction of hair growth. Leave the white of the paper untouched for the lightest areas of white fur. This dog's fur is long and silky and does not cling to the body like some dog fur. On the tongue, shape and darken it a little more with a mix of Cadmium Red Medium Hue and Burnt Umber Light. Use this same mix and a no. 12 round in the insides of the ears and to paint the heart tag on the collar.

4 Mix a little more Burnt Umber Light into the mix used for the heart tag and shade the heart tag. Shade the loop that attaches to the collar with Payne's Gray and Burnt Umber Light on a no. 4 round. Load a no. 4 round with Titanium White and highlight the heart tag, the tongue, the nose and the eyes. With transparent Raw Umber on a no. 4 round, emphasize some of the shadow areas with delicate little hair strokes. Load a no. 4 round with Titanium White and pull some hairs overlapping the eyes. Add some Titanium White to any areas that are too dark.

Around the muzzle, shade the fur with a little Raw Sienna on a no. 4 round, following the downward curve of this fur. Shade around the feet with thinned Raw Umber. Mix a little Burnt Umber Light and Raw Sienna and glaze around the feet. If any area of the dog gets too dark, you can go back into it with Titanium White and re-establish the white fur and lighter areas.

ginger-striped kitten

Color Palette

Golden Fluid Acrylics: Payne's Gray, Raw Sienna, Burnt Sienna, Cadmium Red Medium Hue, Burnt Umber Light.
Liquitex Acrylic Artist Colors: Titanium White.

1 Transfer the drawing onto your paper. Apply the masking film and cut around the kitten. Peel away excess film so the background is exposed and the kitten is covered. Wet the background with clean water using a 3/4-inch (19mm) flat. With the same brush, loosely apply Payne's Gray to the background. While this is still wet, apply more Payne's Gray underneath the kitten as a cast shadow. Let dry.

Next, remove masking film from the kitten. Wet the kitten with clean water and a no. 12 round. Working wet-into-wet, basecoat the ginger-colored areas of the cat with Raw Sienna. Let this color bleed softly out into the white areas. Let dry.

Paint the eyes with Burnt Sienna and the nose and the insides of ears with a mix of Raw Sienna and a touch of Cadmium Red Medium Hue. If needed, go back and darken the body where it meets the face and the top of the head with Raw Sienna on a no. 12 round.

2 Make a warm gray with a mix of Payne's Gray and Burnt Umber Light. Using a no. 6 round (or smaller if you prefer), outline the eyes and paint in the pupils. With a thinner mix of these two colors, begin adding washes to create form. Wash above and below the paws; form the base of the ears and the rounded shape of the face. If the edges seem too hard, go in with clean water while the paint is still wet and soften them. Continue painting in the form and shaping the shoulder area, underneath the chin and around the eyes.

With thinned washes of Burnt Umber Light, go back and shape the ears and top of the head, shade under the eyes, indicate the mouth area with featherlight strokes, and add more separation between the head and body. Shade along the top of the back, where the back leg lies over the body, underneath the belly and the rear leg's joint. Shade in the bend of the tail.

3 To begin painting the fur layer, use a 1/4-inch (6mm) filbert grass comb and a brush mix of Titanium White and just a touch of Raw Sienna to warm it up. Using short strokes and following the direction of hair growth, paint the fur along the shape of the cat's body. Allow the hairs to extend beyond the edges.

To begin painting the darker fur areas, use Raw Sienna and the 1/4-inch (6mm) filbert grass comb. Add depth to the fur color in areas along the cat's back and body, around the back leg, and anywhere where the fur is ginger-colored.

The stripes are a mix of Raw Sienna and Burnt Sienna. Pull the stripe hairs in the direction of hair growth with short strokes of the 1/4-inch (6mm) filbert grass comb.

4 The fur on the cat's head is painted the same way as on the body. Switch to a 1/8-inch (3mm) filbert grass comb for these small areas. The stripes on the cat's head are pulled upward, away from the face.

To begin the final details, load a no. 12 round with a mix of Raw Sienna and Cadmium Red Medium Hue. Paint the pads of the paws, darken the insides of the ears, and line the edge of the mouth. Use Burnt Sienna and the no. 6 round to detail the pads, the nose, the eyes and the outsides of the ears.

Load Titanium White on a 1/8-inch (3mm) filbert grass comb. Use a flicking motion of the brush to paint the hairs along the rims of the ears. Do the same along the bridge of the nose.

To refine the fur and make it look soft and smooth, use a 1/8-inch (3mm) filbert grass comb or a no. 4 round and delicate, light strokes to go over all the fur areas with the same colors you used before to lay in the fur. Add a touch of Titanium White to the fur color, if desired, for better coverage. Add extra softness to the nose and inside the ears with a cotton swab and a pastel pencil in any warm red shade. Rub the swab across the tip of the pastel pencil to pick up some color, then use the swab to apply the color to the paper.

With a no. 4 round and Titanium White, dot a reflective highlight in each eye. Pull some delicate hairs overlapping each eye. With thinned Titanium White, add a secondary highlight in the eyes along the lower curve of the pupils.

With the same brush and Titanium White, pull a couple of delicate whiskers above the eyes and then pull several delicate whiskers from the muzzle.

With thinned Burnt Umber Light, separate the toes on the paws.

berries

Color Palette

Winsor & Newton Artists' Water Colours: Winsor Yellow, Winsor Blue (Green Shade), Brown Madder, Winsor Red, Permanent Alizarin Crimson, Payne's Gray, Yellow Ochre, Permanent Sap Green, Raw Umber, Titanium White.

1 Transfer the design onto the paper. Before painting, dot some masking fluid on the strawberries to indicate seeds. Let dry, then use the no. 12 round to basecoat the strawberries with Winsor Yellow.

Next, mix Winsor Yellow and Winsor Blue (Green Shade) and basecoat the strawberry leaf. The blackberry and raspberry leaves are a mix of Permanent Sap Green and Winsor Blue (Green Shade). You can introduce a little Brown Madder along the edge, if you wish. Finally, paint the raspberries with a mix of Winsor Red and Permanent Alizarin Crimson, and the blackberries with Payne's Gray. The flower center is Yellow Ochre.

2 Mix Permanent Sap Green and Winsor Blue (Green Shade) and use the no. 12 round to paint the shadow side of each leaf. With the same colors, paint a shadow along the side of the stem and indicate little thorns. Paint the strawberries with a wash of Winsor Red. While still wet, drop in some Permanent Alizarin Crimson along the shadow side.

Shade the blackberries with Payne's Grey and shade the raspberries with Permanent Alizarin Crimson. Shade the strawberry flower with Yellow Ochre. Let dry and then shade with Winsor Blue (Green Shade).

3 Wipe out some of the highlights with clean water on the brush. Use a no. 4 round to outline each little round segment of the raspberry with Permanent Alizarin Crimson mixed with a touch of Payne's Gray. Do the same with the blackberry, using Payne's Gray. Glaze a little Brown Madder along the stems. Place the leaf veins with a mix of Permanent Sap Green and Payne's Gray; draw out the line of the vein and then blend it out with clean water on the brush.

4 Remove the masking fluid from the strawberry seeds. Paint the seeds with Yellow Ochre and outline them with Permanent Alizarin Crimson. Soften the outline with clean water. Use Raw Umber to detail the strawberry flower. Add a little highlight on the strawberries and the leaf with Titanium White. You can add a glaze of Winsor Yellow to the leaf to brighten it, if desired.

Shade each round berry segment with the same colors used to outline it (see step 3). Add a highlight of Titanium White to some of the round sections. Mix Permanent Sap Green with a touch of Permanent Alizarin Crimson and add a few more details to the leaves before highlighting with a little Titanium White. Add a few more glazes of Brown Madder to the edges of the leaves, if desired.

Tip

Shading and highlighting help give objects a three-dimensional form. Highlights can also add shine and make fruits and berries look fresh and juicy.

flowers

Color Palette

Winsor & Newton Artists' Water Colours: Permanent Sap Green, Winsor Yellow, Permanent Alizarin Crimson, Burnt Umber, Olive Green, Winsor Violet, Winsor Red, Sepia, Winsor Blue (Green Shade), Yellow Ochre, French Ultramarine, Titanium White.

1 Transfer the design onto the paper. Basecoat the tulip stem leaf with Permanent Sap Green, using the no. 12 round. On the tulip petals, work one at a time and basecoat with Winsor Yellow. Then run some Permanent Alizarin Crimson up the middle while the paint is still wet. Add some Permanent Sap Green at the bottom.

Paint the black-eyed Susan petals with Winsor Yellow, the center with Burnt Umber and the stem with Olive Green. The leaf is basecoated with Winsor Yellow.

Paint the primrose center with Winsor Yellow. Let dry, then paint the petals with Winsor Violet. The leaf is Olive Green with Permanent Sap Green dropped into the center while the Olive Green is still wet.

2 Shade the stem and the inside of the tulip leaf with a wash of Permanent Alizarin Crimson, using the no. 4 round. Mix Winsor Yellow with a little Winsor Red to shade the tulip petals. Shade the bottom of the tulip petals with Permanent Sap Green and a touch of Permanent Alizarin Crimson.

Shade the black-eyed Susan petals with a mix of Winsor Yellow and a little Winsor Red. Stipple the center of the black-eyed Susan with Sepia. Paint a wash of Permanent Sap Green over the leaf. While the leaf is still wet, add a darker green mix of Winsor Blue (Green Shade) and Permanent Sap Green to the center.

Shade the center of the primrose with Yellow Ochre. Shade the petals with a mix of Winsor Violet and French Ultramarine. Lift the center vein out of the primrose leaf with clean water on the brush.

3 Lift out the leaf veins on the black-eyed Susan leaf with clean water on the brush. Shade the stem with a mix of Permanent Sap Green and Permanent Alizarin Crimson. Add the final details to the black-eyed Susan petals with Yellow Ochre. Mix Winsor Yellow and Titanium White together and add dots of pollen to the top of the black-eyed Susan center. Glaze a bit of Permanent Alizarin Crimson on the leaf.

Mix Permanent Sap Green and Permanent Alizarin Crimson and detail the tulip leaf and stem. Lift out some of the highlights on the tulip petals with clean water on the brush, then glaze some Winsor Yellow over the leaf. Add a couple of strokes of Permanent Alizarin Crimson up the center of each petal.

Shade the primrose leaf with a mix of Permanent Sap Green and Permanent Alizarin Crimson. Lift out highlights with clean water on the brush.

stone & wood

Color Palette

Golden Fluid Acrylics: Raw Umber, Payne's Gray, Quinacridone Gold, Burnt Umber Light.
Liquitex Acrylic Artist Colors: Titanium White.

1

2

3

1 With Raw Umber, basecoat an irregular circle for the stone and a vertical rectangle for the wood, using vertical strokes with the 3/4-inch (19mm) flat.

2 To create the stone, crumple up plastic wrap and dip it into Raw Umber paint. Then stamp it onto the basecoated Raw Umber in a natural-looking, random pattern.

To create the wood, use the 1/4-inch (6mm) filbert grass comb (a fan brush can also be used, especially on large areas) and Raw Umber to paint the strokes of wood grain. The wood grain should be spaced irregularly. Feel free to add occasional knots or other imperfections in the wood. Let dry.

3 Create a warm, opaque gray with a mix of Raw Umber, Payne's Gray and a touch of Titanium White. Using the stamped impressions on the stone as a guide, paint the opaque gray around the impressions. On the wood, darken some of the grain lines with a mix of Raw Umber and Payne's Gray, using the no. 12 round. With the same gray mix used on the stone, paint the lighter areas of the wood grain to achieve a weathered look.

4 To shade the stone, use a 3/4-inch (19mm) flat to glaze with Raw Umber and Paynes Gray around the bottom and edges of the stone. Let dry. Highlight the center with a mix of Raw Umber, Payne's Gray and Titanium White. Glaze a little of the Quinacridone Gold along the bottom and sides of the stone to add warmth.

For the wood, glaze with a mix of Burnt Umber Light and Raw Umber. Use the chisel edge of the 3/4-inch (19mm) flat to add occasional diagonal "imperfections." Use the no. 12 round and a mix of Raw Umber and Titanium White to add some small vertical strokes. Add a couple little specks using a mix of Payne's Gray and Raw Umber.

4

making friends

In this painting I used lighting, as well as a warm color palette, to help emphasize the relationship between these two farm babies. The animals are positioned in a beam of light that creates almost a spotlight, while the rest of the scene fades into darkness.

Color Palette: Golden Fluid Acrylics

Raw Umber   Raw Sienna   Burnt Umber Light   Burnt Sienna   Cadmium Yellow Medium Hue

Payne's Gray   Yellow Ochre   Cadmium Red Medium Hue   Titanium White

Brushes: Silver
- Ultra Mini 2431S Designer Round nos. 12 and 6
- Cole Dry Blending Brush 2100S no. 5
- Golden Natural Flat 2008S 3/4-inch (19mm) and 1/2-inch (13mm)
- Ruby Satin 2528S Filbert Grass Combs 1/8-inch (3mm) and 1/4-inch (6mm)

Other Supplies:
- 11" x 14" (28cm x 36cm) sheet of Strathmore 500 series 3-ply bristol board (or illustration board, if you prefer not to stretch your paper)
- foamcore board
- Golden White Absorbent Ground (optional)
- graphite transfer paper
- craft knife
- masking film
- sharp pencil
- drafting tape
- wet palette
- water container

© maday

Prepare for Painting

Enlarge the pattern at 118%. Trace and transfer the pattern to the bristol board, taped securely to the foamcore board. Apply the masking film, and smooth out the bubbles.

1 Paint the Background

Cut the masking film around the wall, the lamb and the kitten, and uncover the background. Paint the background with Burnt Umber Light, using the 3/4-inch (19mm) flat brush. Let dry, then paint the dark area with a Raw Umber/Payne's Gray mix. It may take more than one coat.

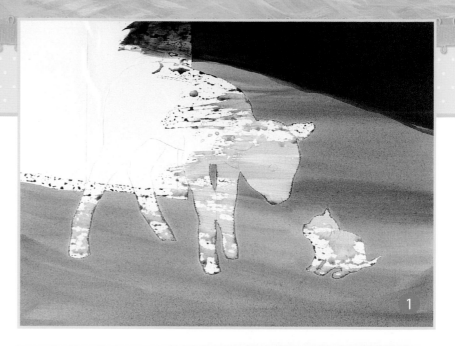

2 Develop the Straw

Begin developing the straw. The darkest tones are a mix of Burnt Umber Light and Yellow Ochre, the midtones are Yellow Ochre, and the lightest areas are a mix of Yellow Ochre, Cadmium Yellow Medium Hue and Titanium White. Use the no. 12 round brush and slip-slap strokes.

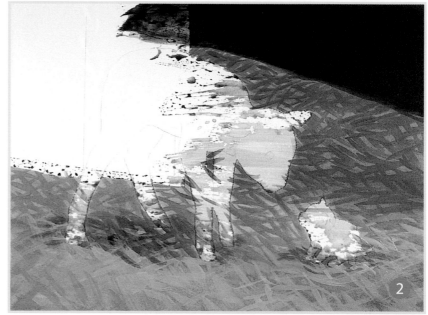

3 Continue Developing the Straw

Build up an opaque layer of straw with a mix of Yellow Ochre/Titanium White, still using the no. 12 round brush, but with more refined strokes.

Tip

A shadow is not a solid mass, so it's better to create shading with transparent glazes. Conversely, light areas look better if they are painted opaquely.

4 Add Glazes to the Straw

Go back to the 3/4-inch (19mm) flat brush, and add transparent glazes to the straw, using Raw Umber for the background, Burnt Umber Light for the midground, and Cadmium Yellow Medium Hue for the lightest areas. Remove the masking film from the wall and basecoat with Raw Umber.

5 Start on the Wall

Using the 1/2-inch (13mm) flat brush, glaze Raw Sienna on the light side of the wall, Raw Umber in the middle of the wall, and a Raw Umber/Payne's Gray mix on the shadow side. Let dry, then switch to the no. 6 round brush and paint the spaces between the boards with the Raw Umber/Payne's Gray mix. Finally, paint the wood grain, using Raw Umber and the 1/4-inch (6mm) filbert grass comb brush.

6 Add Detail to the Wood

Add more wood grain with a mix of Raw Umber/Titanium White. When dry, glaze more washes over the wood with Raw Sienna in the light areas and Raw Umber in the shadowed areas. Bring a few pieces of straw up over the bottom of the wall, and you are ready to remove the masking film from the lamb.

7 Begin Shading the Lamb

Use White Absorbent Ground to touch up places where the paint seeped under the masking film. This product works better than painting over the areas with white paint. It is almost like adding another layer of liquid paper to the surface. Let dry, then shade the lamb first with washes of Raw Umber, then add a little Raw Sienna. The eye is Burnt Umber Light.

8 Add Texture to the Fleece

With the no. 6 round, paint the fleece texture in the shaded areas of the lamb, using very thin Raw Umber. You do not need to put texture in the light areas. Mix Raw Sienna with Cadmium Red Medium Hue and paint the inside of the ears, the nose and the mouth. Give the eye a Payne's Gray pupil, a white highlight, and bring some delicate white lashes down overlapping the eye slightly.

9 Continue Developing the Fleece

Now take some white paint and develop the fleece some more. I used the no. 5 Silver Cole dry blending brush, and tapped on the paint as if I were stippling it. Let the white dry, then add another glaze in the shadows with a Raw Umber/Raw Sienna mix. Tighten up any of the details on the face, and add a few pieces of straw around the feet.

Remove the masking film from the kitten and touch up any areas of paint seepage, using the White Absorbent Ground. If you decide to use white paint instead, use Liquitex's Titanium White, as it covers easily.

10 Basecoat the Kitten

Basecoat the ginger areas of the kitten with Raw Sienna. The eye is Burnt Umber Light.

11 Finish the Lamb

At this point, I realized that I hadn't paid enough attention to the lamb's anatomy when shading. I fixed the back leg by changing the shadow between the leg and tummy, and adding more white fleece to cover the original shading. The beauty of acrylic paint is that you can correct mistakes with ease.

12 Add Form and Shading to the Kitten

Develop the kitten with washes of Burnt Sienna. Add form and shading with Raw Umber.

13 Finish the Kitten

Finish the kitten by painting an opaque layer of fur with the 1/8-inch (3mm) filbert grass comb and a Burnt Sienna/Titanium White mix. Let dry, then glaze over it with thin Burnt Sienna. Switch to the no. 6 round brush (or smaller) and paint some white fur details with Titanium White.

14 Add Final Touches

Finish the painting by bringing some straw up over the kitten, and tweaking any areas you think necessary. Add some highlights to the straw with a Cadmium Yellow Medium Hue/Titanium White mix around the animals to emphasize that they are in a patch of light.

Tip

For extra softness on the lamb, try rubbing a cotton swab across the tip of a pastel pencil. Use the pigment you pick up onto the swab to rub a little soft color onto the paper.

good buddies

In this painting of two farmyard friends, I wanted to show the comfortable relationship between two lifelong pals. I emphasized the warm feeling of friendship by using warm colors throughout the painting. The gray tones in the background wall contrast with the yellows and oranges and help them stand out. I used large pumpkins instead of small ones, because I didn't want the composition to look choppy.

Color Palette: *Golden Fluid Acrylics*

Raw Umber	Raw Sienna	Burnt Umber Light	Burnt Sienna	Cadmium Yellow Medium Hue
Payne's Gray	Yellow Ochre	Cadmium Red Medium Hue	Titanium White	Jenkins Green
Green Gold	Chromium Oxide Green	Vat Orange	Sap Green Permanent	

Brushes: *Silver*
- Ultra Mini 2431S Designer Rounds nos. 12, 6 and 2
- Golden Natural Flat 2008S 3/4-inch (19mm)

Other Supplies:
- 11" x 14" (28cm x 36cm) sheet of Strathmore 500 series 3-ply bristol board
- foamcore board
- craft knife
- masking film
- wet palette
- water container

Prepare for Painting

Enlarge the pattern at 139%. Tape the bristol board to the foam-core support, transfer the pattern, and apply the masking film. Cut around the design and remove the masking film from the background wall. Don't forget the nooks and crannies between the ivy leaves!

1 Basecoat the Background

Basecoat the background with a transparent wash of Burnt Umber Light. I used the 3/4-inch (19mm) flat brush and up-and-down strokes. Switch to the no. 12 round brush. Mix Payne's Gray and Raw Umber together and paint the spaces between the boards. Next, paint the wood grain with a mix of Raw Umber and Burnt Umber Light.

2 Paint the Light Parts of the Wood

Mix Titanium White with Raw Umber and paint the light portions of the wood.

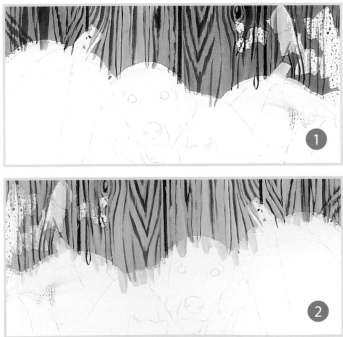

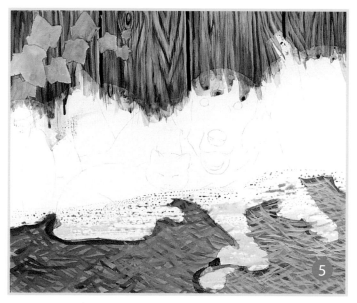

3 Add Glazes to Define the Wood

Continue defining the wood by adding glazes of Burnt Umber Light, Raw Umber and Payne's Gray. Let dry, then add texture with Raw Umber on the 1/4-inch (6mm) filbert grass comb brush. If the wood looks too dark, add lighter streaks with the Raw Umber/Titanium White mix. Let dry, then remove the masking film from the ivy and the ground.

4 Basecoat the Ground

Basecoat the ground with Raw Umber. The ivy receives a basecoat of Sap Green Permanent. After the ground is dry, add some shadows with Raw Umber mixed with a little Payne's Gray.

5 Begin Painting the Straw

Begin building up the straw on the ground, using the no. 12 round brush. Start with Burnt Umber Light. Let dry, then add layers of Yellow Ochre, then Yellow Ochre mixed with Titanium White and Cadmium Yellow Medium Hue.

6 Add Shadows and Highlights to the Straw

Finish the straw by glazing shadows with Raw Umber, and continue adding highlighted clumps of hay with the Titanium White/Yellow Ochre/Cadmium Yellow Medium Hue mix. Remember that the straw is not flat like a carpet; it should have peaks and valleys, created by shadows and highlights.

7 Begin Shading the Ivy

Now we will tend to the ivy before moving on to the pumpkins. Begin by shading where the leaves overlap with a glaze of Jenkins Green. Create a dark green by mixing a little Payne's Gray with some Jenkins Green. Using a no. 12 round, paint the centers of the leaves, blending out to the edges.

8 Detail the Ivy and Basecoat the Pumpkins

Use Green Gold mixed with Titanium White and a no. 6 round brush to add the leaf veins, highlights, and the vine. Let the Green Gold dry, then glaze some Burnt Umber Light onto the leaves. At this point, I felt the wall needed to be knocked back a bit, so I did another Payne's Gray glaze.

Remove the masking film from the background pumpkins. The midground pumpkin, the animals and the apples remain covered. Basecoat the pumpkins with a mix of Vat Orange and Cadmium Yellow Medium Hue, using the no. 12 round brush. The stems are painted with a Chromium Oxide Green/Green Gold mix.

9 Shade the Pumpkin with Glazes

Build form on the pumpkins by shading with layers of glazes. I used Sap Green Permanent, Burnt Sienna, Vat Orange and Cadmium Yellow Medium Hue. For the stem, I used Jenkins Green and Raw Umber. Make sure each glaze is dry before you paint on top of it; you can speed up the process with a hair dryer.

10 Finish the Pumpkins

Glaze some Titanium White highlights on the pumpkins. Bring some straw up over the bottom of the pumpkin on the right. Now remove the masking film from the dog. His scarf remains covered.

11 Basecoat the Dog

Basecoat the dog with Raw Sienna on a no. 12 round. Let dry, then begin shading with a Raw Umber/Raw Sienna mix. Give the ears a glaze of Burnt Umber Light. The lips are a Raw Umber/Payne's Gray mix, and the tongue is a combination of Cadmium Red Medium Hue, Yellow Ochre and Titanium White. Add an extra glaze of green to the pumpkin to help it contrast with the dog.

12 Detail the Dog's Features

With a no. 6 round, use a Payne's Gray/Raw Umber mix, quite dark, for the pupils, the outlines of the eyes, and the details of the nose. Glaze the nose with Burnt Umber Light. Shade the tongue with glazes of a Raw Umber/Cadmium Red Medium Hue mixture. Add highlights with Titanium White. Give the eyes a secondary highlight with a Raw Sienna/Titanium White mix.

13 Add Texture to the Fur

Remove the masking film from the remaining pumpkin and basecoat as before. Finish painting the pumpkin using the same colors and techniques as before. Remove the masking film from the bandanna and basecoat it with a Cadmium Red Medium Hue/Yellow Ochre mix. Now pick up the 1/4-inch (6mm) filbert grass comb brush and start developing the dog's fur, using a mix of Raw Sienna and Titanium White. As always, paint in the direction of hair growth.

14 Glaze the Fur

Switch back to the no. 6 round brush, and glaze the dog's fur, using separate washes of Raw Sienna, Burnt Umber, Burnt Sienna, and Raw Umber. Begin adding shape to the scarf with Burnt Sienna shadows and White highlights.

15 Complete the Dog

Finish the dog with a final opaque layer of fur, using the no. 6 brush and the previous colors, with the addition of Titanium White. Labradors have very short fur, so you will need to make short, dabbing strokes with your brush. I used the no. 6 for the face and the 1/8-inch (3mm) grass comb for the body. Now finish the scarf with Titanium White details. If you don't want to do a bandanna pattern, you could try polka dots, stripes or even little hearts. Remove all the remaining masking film.

16 Basecoat the Cat

Basecoat the cat with Raw Umber as shown, leaving the white areas as plain paper. The apples are painted with Cadmium Yellow Medium Hue. This will shine through the subsequent layers of paint and give the apples a warm glow.

17 Add Color to the Apples and Cat

Wet the apples with clean water. While they are wet, drop in some Green Gold mixed with a little Sap Green Permanent, and then some Cadmium Red Medium Hue mixed with a little Burnt Sienna. Paint the darks on the cat with Raw Umber, and glaze a little Burnt Sienna in some areas.

18 Build Opaque Layer of Fur

Build up an opaque layer of fur with a mix of Raw Umber and Titanium White, using the 1/4-inch (6mm) grass comb. Shade and highlight the apples, using the no. 6 round brush and a combination of Cadmium Red Medium Hue and Sap Green Permanent. Highlight with Titanium White.

19 Detail the Apples and Cat

Finish detailing the apples with Raw Umber stems, and add pieces of straw to overlap. Switch to the no. 2 round brush and begin detailing the cat, using Raw Umber, Raw Sienna, Burnt Sienna, and a very dark brown mixed from Raw Umber and Payne's Gray. The photo shows this in progress.

20 Add the Final Details

Glaze a little more shadow to the bandanna with a Cadmium Medium Hue Red/Payne's Gray mix. Add more details to the cat with Raw Umber, using the no. 2 brush and tiny strokes. Use Titanium White for the lightest hairs, including the whiskers. If you are nervous about painting the whiskers' fine lines, you can either leave them out, or try scratching them out carefully with the tip of your craft knife. I decided at the last minute that the painting would benefit from adding another apple by the cat, so the areas of red would lead your eye around the painting. The beauty of acrylic is that you can add details as you go. For overpainting, I prefer to use the Titanium White made by Liquitex.

Detail of the Cat

happy puppy

Don't you love how a puppy seems to smile with an open mouth and lolling tongue? I just couldn't resist painting this happy little fellow. I placed him against the cool gray stones so that his warm fur would really stand out.

Color Palette: Golden Fluid Acrylics

Yellow Ochre	Green Gold	Jenkins Green	Chromium Oxide Green	Raw Umber

Quinacridone Gold	Quinacridone Crimson	Raw Sienna	Burnt Umber Light	Titanium White

Payne's Gray	Cadmium Red Medium Hue	Cadmium Yellow Medium Hue

Brushes: Silver
- Ultra Mini 2431S Designer Rounds nos. 12 and 6
- Cole Dry Blending Brush 2100S no. 5
- Golden Natural Flat 2008S 3/4-inch (19mm)
- Ruby Satin 2528S Filbert Grass Combs 1/4-inch (6mm) and 1/8-inch (3mm)

Other Supplies:
- 11" x 14" (28cm x 36cm) sheet of Strathmore 500 series 3-ply bristol board
- foamcore board
- craft knife
- masking film
- wet palette
- water container
- drafting tape
- sharp pencil
- graphite transfer paper
- plastic cling wrap
- small sponge roller about 2" (5cm) long (available at craft shops in the stenciling section)

Prepare for Painting

Enlarge the pattern at 116%. Trace and transfer the pattern to your bristol board. Prepare the surface as instructed in Part One, "Getting Started." Apply the masking film.

1 Paint the Background

Once you have transferred the design and applied the masking film, cut around the design. Peel away the masking film covering the background. Wet the background with clean water, then apply Yellow Ochre with the sponge roller. Don't worry if it isn't smooth. You could also use the flat brush for this step if you prefer.

2 Deepen the Background Color

Wet the surface again. With the roller, roll on Jenkins Green first, concentrating on the edges. Add some Raw Umber to the green at the upper corners. Wipe the excess paint off the roller, then add Quinacridone Gold to the no. 12 round brush and use slip-slap strokes. Work wet-in-wet, a section at a time, and blend strokes of Raw Umber, a Raw Umber/Titanium White 1:2 mix and Yellow Ochre.

3 Paint the Stones

Basecoat the stones with Raw Umber and the no. 12 round brush. Paint some loose leaf and grass shapes behind the flowers in the container, using Chromium Oxide Green, Green Gold, Quinacridone Gold, and Quinacridone Gold mixed with Titanium White. Next, crumple up some plastic cling wrap into a pad. Dip the pad into Raw Umber and use it to stamp texture onto the stones.

4 Add Form to the Stones

Mix up a medium gray with Raw Umber, Payne's Gray and Titanium White. Begin adding form to the stones, following shapes you see in the stamped Raw Umber marks. Use your imagination! Add shadows between the stones with a darker Raw Umber/Payne's Gray mix.

5 Continue Painting the Stones

Still using the no. 12 round brush, continue building up the stones with varying shades of gray. When this is dry, glaze a little Chromium Oxide Green and Quinacridone Gold in some areas. Now remove the masking film from the ground.

6 Paint the Ground

Basecoat the ground with Raw Umber and a 3/4-inch (19mm) flat. Let dry. Start building up the ground, using the no. 12 round brush and slip-slap strokes. Work wet-in-wet, a section at a time, and blend strokes of Raw Umber, a Raw Umber/Titanium White 1:2 mix, and Yellow Ochre. Make sure to add shadows under the puppy, flowers, etc. Finally, add a few pieces of straw to the ground with a Yellow Ochre/Titanium White mix. The photo shows this in progress. Let dry, then remove the masking film from the flowers and leaves, except for the flowers that overlap the planter barrel.

7 Begin the Leaves and Flowers

With the no. 12 round, basecoat the clover leaves with Jenkins Green, and the flowers with a mixture of Quinacridone Crimson and Titanium White. Let dry, then add a little Chromium Oxide Green to the clover centers. The daisy leaves are a 1:2 mix of Jenkins Green and Green Gold. The daisy centers are Cadmium Yellow Medium Hue. The stems are a Chromium Oxide Green/Titanium White mix.

8 Add Blades of Grass

Switch to the no. 6 round brush, and mix Titanium White, Green Gold and Jenkins Green, and paint some blades of grass behind the stones. Mix Titanium White with Quinacridone Gold and paint some dry weeds and grasses.

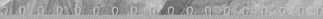

9 Finish the Clover Leaves

Using the no. 6 round brush, paint the clover petals with a light pink mixed from Cadmium Red Medium Hue and Titanium White. Detail with Quinacridone Crimson. For the leaves, mix Titanium White with Jenkins Green and paint the light "arrow" shape on each leaf. Detail with Jenkins Green, and glaze some of the leaves with Green Gold.

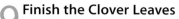

10 Detail the Grass and Flowers

Detail the background grasses with Jenkins Green and a Quinacridone Gold/Yellow Ochre mix. Highlight with a Green Gold/Titanium White mix. Add Burnt Umber Light for the deepest darks. Begin shading the daisies by stippling some Raw Sienna into the centers with the dry blending brush. Glaze a little Green Gold and Raw Sienna where the petals meet the center, and start shading the petals with a warm gray mixed from Raw Umber and Payne's Gray.

11 Begin Painting the Planter Barrel

Basecoat the wooden staves with a wash of Burnt Umber Light. The circular bands get a basecoat of Payne's Gray. Shade the barrel with a little Raw Umber on the staves, and a Raw Umber/Payne's Gray mix for the bands.

12 Add Texture to the Planter

Finish the planter by adding wood grain texture to the staves, using the 1/4-inch (6mm) filbert grass comb and Raw Umber. Add any additional glazes for shading, if desired, using the no. 6 round brush.

13 Finish the Planter

Drybrush some highlights over the top, using Raw Umber mixed with a little Titanium White. Highlight the bands with a light gray made from Raw Umber, Titanium White and Payne's Gray. Let dry, then add a few glazes of Raw Umber to "age" it a bit.

14 Basecoat the Puppy

Remove the masking film from the puppy, and basecoat. Paint the body with Raw Sienna, Burnt Umber Light for the eyes and nose, Raw Umber for the lips, and Cadmium Red Medium Hue for the tongue. Let dry, then begin detailing. Mix a black from Payne's Gray and Raw Umber, and use it to paint the pupils of the eyes, the nose and around the mouth. Detail the eyes and tongue with Raw Umber, and add highlights with Titanium White. Load the 1/4-inch (6mm) filbert grass comb with Burnt Umber Light and begin adding a little form to the fur.

15 Finish the Flowers

Detail the daisy leaves with a mix of Jenkins Green and Chromium Oxide Green. Highlight with a Green Gold/Titanium White mix, and add a few glazes of Quinacridone Crimson to add depth to the darkest areas. Finish shading and detailing the daisies with the same gray as before. Use a delicate hand here; you don't have to detail every petal. Paint the remaining clover as before.

16 Build Up and Refine the Fur

Continue building up the puppy's fur, using a mix of Raw Sienna and Titanium White and the 3/8-inch (10mm) filbert grass comb. Always stroke in the direction of fur growth.

Using glazes, continue painting the puppy's fur. Switch back to the no. 6 round brush and paint with tiny, delicate strokes to refine the fur. Just keep adding fur strokes until it looks smooth and soft. As you'll discover, it is easy to keep adding layers for ages!

Finish the painting by adding details to the loose bits of straw on the ground, using Yellow Ochre, Raw Umber and Chromium Oxide Green.

Detail of Planter Flowers

acrylic demonstration

berry cute

I don't know which is sweeter in this painting, the kitten's face or the berries in which she nestles! If you need more in depth instruction, refer back to the mini-demos at the beginning of this section. Try to keep the fur brushstrokes soft rather than coarse, just like a kitty's fur.

Color Palette: *Golden Fluid Acrylics*

Yellow Ochre	Green Gold	Raw Umber	Payne's Gray
Jenkins Green	Burnt Sienna	Quinacridone Crimson	Burnt Umber Light
Chromium Oxide Green	Cobalt Blue	Titanium White	

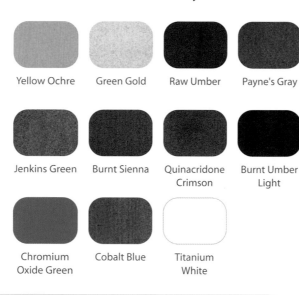

Brushes: Silver
- Ultra Mini 2431S Designer Round nos. 12, 6 and 2
- Golden Natural Flat 2008S 3/4-inch (19mm)
- Cole Dry Blending Brush 2100S round no. 5
- Ruby Satin 2528S Filbert Grass Combs in 1/4-inch (6mm) and 1/8-inch (3mm)

Other Supplies:
- 9" x 12" (23cm x 30cm) Canson Montval watercolor block
- wet palette
- water container
- graphite transfer paper
- sharp pencil
- masking film
- craft knife
- kneaded eraser
- sea sponge

Prepare for Painting

This is a very busy design and it's important to prepare the paper properly. Enlarge the pattern at 127%. After tracing and transferring the pattern, soften any dark lines with the kneaded eraser. Apply the masking film and cut to expose the background. Make sure you get all the nooks and crannies between the leaves!

1 Paint the Background

Wet the background with clear water, and apply a Yellow Ochre wash, using the 3/4-inch (19mm) flat brush. Dry completely, then use a sponge to pat more Yellow Ochre over the top. This will help add texture and depth to the background.

2 Paint Leaf Shapes

Time to loosen up and get messy! Wet the background again and paint with a 1:1 mix of Green Gold and Jenkins Green. Gradually add more Jenkins Green as you move down the painting. While it is still wet, paint loose background leaf shapes. Add a little Quinacridone Crimson to the darkest shapes. Let dry.

3 Add Blue Around the Leaf Shapes

Mix some Cobalt Blue with Titanium White at about 3:1. Using the paint very thin and watery, add the blue to the top of the painting, painting around the leaf shapes when possible. Now, carefully remove the masking film from the background leaves. If you encountered minor seepage under the masking film as a result of painting so wet, lift the masking film gently or it could tear the paper underneath.

Tip

When mixing colors, always mix a little of the stronger color into the weaker color. Gradually add more of the stronger color until you have the mix you desire.

4 Basecoat the Background Leaves

Using the no. 12 round, basecoat the background leaves with varying mixes of Green Gold and Jenkins Green. Some should be darker than others. While the leaves are still wet, drop in some Burnt Sienna or Yellow Ochre along some of the edges. The stems are a mix of Burnt Sienna and Green Gold.

5 Shade and Highlight the Leaves

Shade one side of each leaf with Jenkins Green. Let dry, then paint the leaf veins with Jenkins Green mixed with a little Quinacridone Crimson. Create highlights with Titanium White. The picture shows the leaves at different stages: some basecoated, some shaded and some highlighted.

6 Glaze to Deepen Shadows

Glaze some of the highlights with Green Gold and some with

Yellow Ochre. Use a glaze of Quinacridone Crimson to deepen some shadows. Now remove the masking film from the next layer of leaves and berries. Paint the leaves as before, and basecoat the berries with Quinacridone Crimson. Switch to the no. 6 round brush and start creating blades of grass with a mix of Jenkins Green/Green Gold/Titanium White. Detail with a mix of Jenkins Green/Cobalt Blue.

7 Shade and Highlight the Raspberries

With the no. 6 round brush, begin shading the berries with another glaze of Quinacridone Crimson. When dry, start defining each little segment with a dark red mixed from Quinacridone Crimson and a little Jenkins Green. Continue shading each segment, then add a Titanium White highlight to some of them. The photograph shows the raspberries at several stages, from shading to highlights.

8 Basecoat the Kitten

Now remove the masking film from the kitten. With a no. 12 round brush, basecoat using a warm gray made from Burnt Umber Light and Payne's Gray. Add more Burnt Umber for the inside of the ears. The nose is a mix of Quinacridone Crimson and Burnt Umber Light, and the eyes are Green Gold and Yellow Ochre.

9 Paint the Eyes and Shade the Body

Using the no. 6 round brush, begin with the eyes. Mix a little Burnt Umber Light with Jenkins Green and paint the edges of the eyeballs, blending toward the center. Now, mix up a black with Payne's Gray and Burnt Umber; outline the eyes and add pupils. Add Titanium White highlights and a few touches of Burnt Umber Light, and the eyes are done for the moment. Now add some shading to the kitten's body with glazes of the Burnt Umber Light/Payne's Gray mix. Add a touch of Quinacridone Crimson to kitty's ears.

10 Fluff the Fur

It's time to build up some fur with your filbert grass comb brushes. Start with the 1/4-inch (6mm) brush and an opaque gray made by adding Titanium White to your Payne's Gray/Burnt Umber Light mix. Stroke the fur along the kitty's back, always moving in the direction of hair growth. Use various shades of gray, building up the form before you add the white hairs with the 1/8-inch (3mm) filbert grass comb. Refine and smooth the hairs with the no. 6 round. Our kitty looks pretty spiky, but don't worry, we're not through with him yet!

11 Develop the Facial Fur

With the no. 6 round, build up the fur pattern on the face, working from dark to light. Use some Raw Umber to warm up some of the hairs on the face.

12 Continue the Layers of Fur

Continue developing the face with soft hairs. When the face is complete (except for the whiskers), move on to the body. It will take several layers to make this kitten's fur look smooth.

13 Paint More Leaves and Berries

Now remove the masking film from the flowers, the terra-cotta pots and some more leaves. The leaves in front of the flower-pots and the bee should remain covered. Paint the leaves and berries in the same manner as before. Basecoat the pots with Burnt Sienna and Yellow Ochre mixed 1:1 on a no. 12 round brush. Start adding form with Burnt Umber Light.

14 Finish the Flower Pots and Blossoms

Continue shading the pots with Burnt Umber Light and the no. 12 round brush. Use Raw Umber for the darkest areas. Notice how I have left some reflected light along the edges. This helps the pots look round. Switch to the no. 6 round brush and paint the blossoms, using a pale Quinacridone Crimson and Titanium White mix, then shade with Raw Umber. Add Yellow Ochre centers. Finally, basecoat the bee, using Yellow Ochre for the thorax and Raw Umber for the head and abdomen.

15 Antique the Pots

I like plant pots to look as if they've been around for a while, so we're going to "age" ours. Mix some Titanium White with Chromium Oxide Green, and loosely drybrush the pots with the no. 12 round brush. Blend with the dry blending brush. Add more colors, like Raw Umber, and blend them as well. Now you can remove the masking film from the remaining leaves.

16 Add the Final Details

Paint the remaining leaves as before. Now finish the final details. Add Titanium White whiskers with the no. 6 round brush (or a liner brush, if you prefer). Detail the bee with the black you mixed from Burnt Umber Light and Payne's Gray. Add white highlights. For the yellow thorax, detail with Raw Umber. The wings receive touches of Payne's Gray, then a Jenkins Green glaze, as if the leaf were showing through. Finally, draw in the flower stamens with Raw Umber and Jenkins Green. Go through the painting and make any adjustments you like; I added some extra leaf glazes and touched up kitty's eyes.

Framing for Focus

Have you noticed how the berries and flowers make a "frame" around the kitten? This, in combination with the cool gray fur against the warm foliage, helps make our feline friend the star of the show.

briars & butterflies

This shy little fawn hiding among wild roses is a somewhat intricate design and will require a bit of concentration when cutting the masking film. If you persevere, though, I think you will find that the results are worth the effort!

Color Palette: *Golden Fluid Acrylics*

Raw Umber • Payne's Gray • Burnt Umber Light • Jenkins Green • Raw Sienna • Burnt Sienna

Cadmium Red Medium Hue • Ultramarine Blue • Cadmium Yellow Medium Hue • Green Gold • Chromium Oxide Green • Quinacridone Crimson

Vat Orange • Yellow Ochre • Carbon Black • Phthalo Green (blue shade)

Liquitex Acrylic Artist Colors

Titanium White • Sap Green Permanent

Brushes: *Silver*
- Ultra Mini 2431S Designer Round nos. 12, 6 and 2
- Ruby Satin 2528S Filbert Grass Combs 1/4-inch (6mm) and 1/8-inch (3mm)
- Golden Natural Flat 2008S 3/4-inch (19mm)

Other Supplies:
- 11" x 14" (28cm x 36cm) sheet of Strathmore 500 series 3-ply bristol board (or illustration board, if you prefer not to stretch your paper)
- foamcore board
- Golden White Absorbent Ground (optional)
- graphite transfer paper
- craft knife
- masking film
- sharp pencil
- drafting tape
- wet palette
- water container
- sponge roller about 2" (5cm) wide (available at craft shops in the stenciling section)
- sea sponge
- pink colored pencil (optional)
- rubbing alcohol (to clean paint off of masking film)

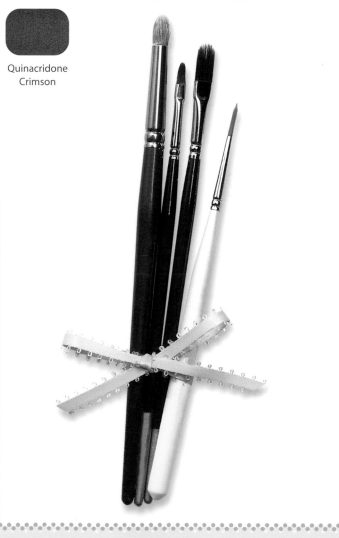

Prepare for Painting

Enlarge the pattern at 112%. Trace and transfer the pattern to the the bristol board. Apply masking film and cut around the design to expose the background. Don't forget all the nooks and crannies between the leaves!

Tip

This painting will take some time to do. If you use a Sta-Wet palette, mist the paint with clean water before you close the lid, wrap it in plastic wrap or a sealed sandwich bag, and place it in the refrigerator. The paint will stay wet almost indefinitely.

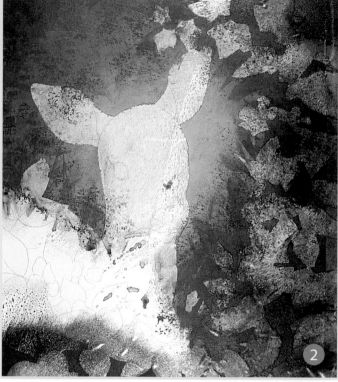

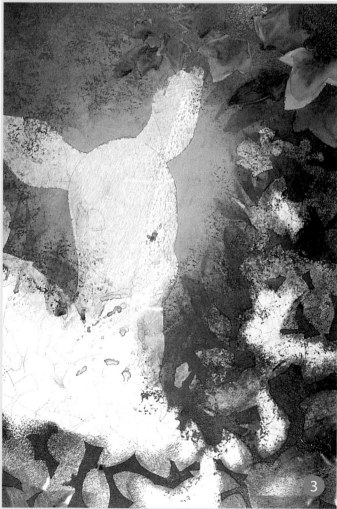

1 Begin Painting the Background

Wet the background with clean water. Put a few drops of paint on the paper: Green Gold in the center, Jenkins Green around the edges, and a little Burnt Sienna where the fawn disappears behind the leaves. Use the sponge roller to spread the paint thinly across the background.

2 Add Texture to the Background

Paint a thin glaze of Jenkins Green over the entire background, using the 3/4-inch (19mm) flat brush. Let dry, then sponge paint some texture onto the background with Jenkins Green, Chromium Oxide Green, Green Gold and Burnt Sienna. Leave a "halo" of light around the fawn's head. Finally, paint a few loose leaf shapes with a mix of Chromium Oxide Green and Green Gold.

3 Begin Painting the Ivy

Remove the masking film from the ivy in the upper right corner. If the masking film is so covered with paint that you can't see the drawing well enough to cut around it, try removing some of the dried paint with rubbing alcohol on a tissue. Basecoat the ivy with a mix of Jenkins Green/Phthalo Green (blue shade), using the no. 12 round brush. Let dry, then paint the centers of the leaves with a glaze of Jenkins Green. Give some of the leaves an additional glaze of Quinacridone Crimson.

4 Develop the Ivy

At this point, add a thin glaze of Burnt Sienna over the background to help the ivy leaves stand out. After it is dry, draw in the stem with a mix of Green Gold/Titanium White. Add form to the leaves with a light mix of Green Gold/Phthalo Green/Titanium White.

5 Continue Developing the Ivy

Switch to the no. 6 round brush. Continue developing the ivy leaves by painting the leaf veins with the Green Gold/Titanium White. Add white highlights and texture between the veins with Sap Green Permanent. You can add more glazes of Quinacridone Crimson, if desired. Glaze the stem with Burnt Sienna. Now remove the masking film from the fawn.

6 Begin Painting the Fawn

Basecoat the fawn with Raw Sienna. The nose is Raw Umber; the eyes are Burnt Umber Light. Leave white paper for the white areas around the eyes and mouth. Begin adding form by glazing the ears with Raw Umber, the head, nose and back with Burnt Umber. Shade the neck with Raw Umber.

7 Develop the Fawn

Add texture to the background with loose, leaflike shapes and slip-slap strokes. Use Jenkins Green, Burnt Umber, Chromium Oxide Green on a no. 12 round brush. Continue adding form to the fawn with Raw Umber. Add a Burnt Sienna glaze to the fawn's back, head and the inside of the ears.

72

8 Develop the Fawn's Features

Remove the masking film from some of the wild rose leaves, and basecoat with Sap Green Permanent. Begin developing the fawn's eyes and nose using Carbon Black. Highlight with Titanium White. Add a dark rim to the eyes with Raw Umber mixed with Carbon Black. Using the no. 6 round or a smaller brush, bring out some white hairs overlapping the eyes a little bit. Add some Raw Umber hairs with a 1/4-inch (6mm) filbert grass comb.

9 Detail the Fur

Using the 1/4-inch (6mm) filbert grass comb, start building up the hairs on the fawn. Use Raw Sienna on the neck, Burnt Sienna on the head and back, and Raw Umber on the ears. Your brushstrokes should follow the direction of fur growth.

10 Add White to the Fur

Start creating an opaque layer of fur by mixing Titanium White in with the Raw Sienna. The chin, neck, inside of the ears, and patch by the nose are pure Titanium White.

11 Add Details to the Fawn

Switch to the no. 12 round and glaze over the opaque layer of fur using Burnt Sienna, Raw Sienna and Raw Umber. Now pick up your no. 6 brush, and start on some details. The spots on the fawn's back are a Raw Sienna/Titanium White mix. The whiskers on her chin are pure white. Add some refining strokes of fur, using the various browns we have previously selected. The details around the eyes are Raw Umber.

73

12 Develop the Rose Leaves

Remove the masking film from more of the wild rose leaves and basecoat with Sap Green Permanent, using the no. 12 round brush. Paint the stems with a mix of Sap Green Permanent/Titanium White. Give the shadow side of the leaves a glaze of a Sap Green Permanent/Jenkins Green mix. Switch to the no. 6 round and paint in the leaf veins with Jenkins Green. The photo at top shows this in progress.

13 Add Glazes to the Rose Leaves

Add glazes of Quinacridone Crimson to the shadow areas on the rose leaves and glazes of Green Gold to the lighter areas. Use Titanium White for highlights. Remove the masking film from everything except the butterflies.

14 Begin Painting the Roses

Paint the remaining leaves as before. Don't forget to add the stems. For a natural look, add some holes and imperfections to the leaves. Touch up any areas where paint may have seeped under the masking film onto the roses with Absorbent Ground. Paint the centers of the roses with Yellow Ochre. Now mix a delicate pink from Titanium White and Cadmium Red Medium Hue. Paint the rose petals, starting at the outer edge and stroking toward the center. Leave some white around the Yellow Ochre center.

15 Shade and Highlight the Flowers

Shade the pink parts of the petals with very thin glazes of Quinacridone Crimson. Shade the white areas with transparent Payne's Gray. Use a no. 6 brush or smaller. The petals have very delicate little veins; you can add these with a very sharp pink colored pencil if you are nervous about putting them in with a brush. Finally, shade the flowers centers with a little Sap Green Permanent; stipple in some highlights with a Titanium White/Cadmium Yellow Medium Hue mix; and finish with Yellow Ochre stamens.

16 Basecoat the Butterflies

Remove the masking film from the butterflies. Basecoat two of the butterflies with Cadmium Yellow Medium Hue mixed with just a touch of Titanium White. The other two butterflies are painted with Ultramarine Blue, also combined with a little Titanium White. The yellow butterflies have Raw Umber bodies, and the blue butterflies' bodies are Payne's Gray. Glaze some Burnt Umber Light onto the wings of all the butterflies, starting where the wing meets the body and blending outwards. Don't go as far as the outer edge of the wings; stop somewhere in the middle.

17 Add Detail to the Butterflies

For the yellow butterflies, glaze a mix of Vat Orange/Cadmium Yellow Medium Hue over the Burnt Umber Light, blending outwards. Paint the rims of the wings with Burnt Umber Light on a no. 6 round or smaller brush. For the blue butterflies, rim the wings with Titanium White, and then add some Burnt Umber Light inside the white edge.

18 Add Final Touches to the Butterflies

Using the no. 2 round brush, add the final details to the butterflies. For the blue butterflies' bodies, detail with Payne's Gray. Mix Payne's Gray with Ultramarine Blue and paint subtle, transparent dots on the wings. The antennae are Payne's Gray mixed with Titanium White. The wing veins are Burnt Umber Light. Switch to a liner brush for the details if it makes you more comfortable.

Detail the yellow butterflies' bodies with Raw Umber. The wing veins and antennae are also Raw Umber. Add spots to the brown wing borders with a Cadmium Yellow Medium Hue/Titanium White mix. Finally, add wing spots with Burnt Umber Light and a Cadmium Red Medium Hue/Burnt Umber Light mix.

three amigos

In this project, we have three curious kittens with different fur patterns and textures. The dark background behind the kittens serves to make them the focal point of the painting, because the greatest contrast is between the dark space and the light fur.

Color Palette: Golden Fluid Acrylics

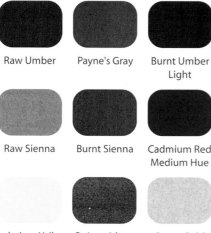

Raw Umber

Payne's Gray

Burnt Umber Light

Jenkins Green

Raw Sienna

Burnt Sienna

Cadmium Red Medium Hue

Ultramarine Blue

Cadmium Yellow Medium Hue

Quinacridone Magenta

Green Gold

Dioxazine Purple

Quinacridone Crimson

Liquitex Acrylic Artist Colors

Sap Green Permanent

Titanium White

Brushes: Silver
- Ultra Mini 2431S Designer Rounds nos. 12, 4 and 2
- Ruby Satin 2528S Filbert Grass Combs 1/8-inch (3mm) and 1/4-inch (6mm)
- Golden Natural Flat 2008S 3/4-inch (19mm)

Other Supplies:
- 11" x 14" (28cm x 36cm) sheet of Strathmore 500 series 3-ply bristol board (or illustration board, if you prefer not to stretch your paper)
- foamcore board
- graphite transfer paper
- craft knife
- masking film
- sharp pencil
- drafting tape
- wet palette
- water container
- dark-green colored pencil and ruler (optional)
- red and white pastel pencils
- cotton swabs
- sea sponge

Prepare for Painting

Enlarge the pattern at 111%. Tape the bristol board to the foamcore support. Trace and transfer the pattern. Apply masking film and cut around the design to expose the background.

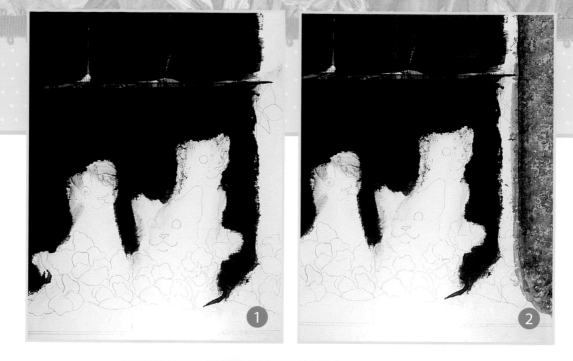

1 Paint the Background

Using the 3/4-inch (19mm) Golden Natural Flat, wet the background with clean water, then basecoat with Burnt Umber Light. Let dry, then paint another coat with a Burnt Umber Light/Payne's Gray mix. It may take more than one coat to achieve a deep, rich background. Clean the masking film with rubbing alcohol on a tissue if it gets covered with too much paint.

2 Paint the Wall

Remove the masking film from the wall at the right, and basecoat with Raw Umber. Let dry, then sponge paint with a medium brown mixed from Raw Umber and Titanium White. Add more Titanium White and sponge paint again. Finally, glaze some Raw Umber along the window frame for a shadow. Add some reflected light to the windows by drawing the lights with a white pastel pencil, then blending with a cotton swab.

3 Paint the Window Frame

Remove the masking film from the window frame, and basecoat with a Jenkins Green/Titanium White mix. Dry thoroughly, then add shading with pure Jenkins Green. Mix in more white for highlights. For the darkest greens, add a touch of Payne's Gray. Add a little glaze of Burnt Umber Light around the edges of the window panes. Let dry. If your lines aren't straight, go in and touch them up with a dark-green colored pencil and a ruler.

4 Begin Painting the Kittens

Carefully lift the masking film off the two kittens on either side of the center. Load your 1/8-inch (3mm) filbert grass comb with Titanium White, and paint the fluffy fur overlapping the outlines. I like the Liquitex Titanium White for this because I find it easier to paint over than the more glossy Golden acrylics version. Basecoat the kitties with Raw Sienna as shown, using the no. 12 round brush.

5 Continue Developing the Kittens

Mix a gray by combining Raw Umber and Payne's Gray, and thin it down with clean water so it is transparent and watery. Use this on a no. 12 round to add shadows and create form on the kittens. Paint the eyes with Sap Green Permanent, let dry, then add a glaze of Ultramarine Blue to the kitty on the left. Add a thin glaze of Cadmium Red Medium Hue to the ears and noses.

6 Develop the Eyes

Mix a warm black from Raw Umber and Payne's Gray and paint the pupils of the eyes, using a no. 4 round or smaller brush. Add touches of Raw Sienna on either side of the pupil. Outline the eyes with the warm black, and blend it into the iris. Add Titanium White dots for highlights, and a thinner stroke of Titanium White as the secondary highlight. Develop the areas around the eyes and nose with Raw Umber. Add another glaze of Raw Sienna mixed with Cadmium Red Medium Hue to the nose, and a soft white highlight.

7 Add Texture to the Fur

For the kitty on the left, mix Raw Sienna with Burnt Sienna for the dark ginger fur. Add more fur with plain Raw Sienna, and develop the shadow areas further with Raw Umber. Switch to the kitten on the right. Define the dark patches of fur with Raw Umber and the light patches with Raw Sienna.

8 Begin Creating the Opaque Fur Layer

Begin creating the opaque fur layer, using the 1/8-inch (3mm) filbert grass comb and a mix of Titanium White and Raw Sienna. Start with the kitten on the left. Once this is dry, glaze over it with Raw Sienna. Go over the white areas of fur with the 1/8-inch (3mm) filbert grass comb and Titanium White. Finally, pick up the no. 2 round brush and add details to the ears and extra white hairs. Go over the whole face and soften and refine the fur with additional glazes of Raw Sienna, Raw Umber and Burnt Sienna. If you wish, rub a cotton swab over a red pastel pencil, and use the swab to soften the nose, mouth and inside the ears. The photo above shows the left kitten finished, while the one on the right has the opaque layer only.

9 Continue Painting the Second Kitten

Continue painting the second kitten in the same manner as the first. Glaze and refine the fur with Raw Umber and Raw Sienna. Add white hairs with the no. 2 round, and detail the ears. Add warmth to the nose, mouth and ears with a cotton swab rubbed on a red pastel pencil. Remove the masking film from the foreground kitten and the butterfly.

10 Begin Painting the Third Kitten

Time for the last kitten. Begin in the same manner as before, by using Titanium White to create fluffy fur edges, then basecoating with Raw Sienna. Notice that this kitten has shorter hair, so your fur strokes can be shorter. Use Raw Umber to begin developing the fur pattern. The eyes are basecoated with Raw Sienna with a glaze of Sap Green Permanent on top.

11 Create the Opaque Fur Layer

Now create the opaque fur layer, using a Raw Umber/ Titanium White mix. The eyes are detailed as you did for the previous kitties in Steps 5 and 6. Glaze over the opaque layer once it is dry, using a mix of Raw Umber/Payne's Gray for the darkest fur, and Raw Sienna for the warmest areas. Smudge some red pastel pencil on the nose and mouth with a cotton swab. Add some white whiskers using the no. 2 round brush or a liner brush if you prefer. Remove the masking film from the flowers, with the exception of the blossoms that overlap the window box.

12 Paint the Flowers and Butterfly

Using the no. 4 round brush and thin, watery paint, basecoat the butterfly with Ultramarine Blue. The body is Payne's Gray. The foreground leaves are painted with Green Gold, and the leaves in shadow are a mix of Green Gold and Sap Green Permanent. Basecoat all the flowers with Quinacridone Magenta. Let dry, then give some of the flowers a glaze of Dioxazine Purple.

13 Add Details to the Leaves

Glaze Jenkins Green over the shadow areas on the leaves, and Sap Green Permanent over the light areas. The paint should be thin, so the Green Gold shines through and give the leaves a warm glow. Use Jenkins Green to paint one side of each leaf darker. Our imaginary light source is at the upper left of this painting, and the leaves should reflect this. Use a Green Gold/Titanium White mix for the center veins of the leaves. Glaze some Ultramarine Blue on the purple pansies and Cadmium Yellow Medium Hue (very thin) on the pink blossoms.

14 Finish Painting the Leaves

Paint a wash of Quinacridone Crimson over the leaf shadows. Using the no. 4 round or a smaller brush, add more leaf veins with the Green Gold/Titanium White mix. Detail between the veins with Sap Green Permanent. Highlight with the Green Gold/Titanium White mix, and deepen the darkest shadows with a mix of Jenkins Green and Ultramarine Blue. Begin delicately shading the pink pansies with Quinacridone Crimson.

15 Add Shading and Highlights to the Flowers

Shade the purple pansies with Dioxazine Purple mixed with Ultramarine Blue. You can use this same color to deepen some of the shading on the pink pansies. Mix Payne's Gray with Quinacridone Crimson and paint the dark lines radiating outward from the center of the pink pansies, using the no. 2 round brush. For the purple pansies, mix Ultramarine Blue and Payne's Gray. To deepen the shadows on the purple flowers, add water to the same mix, so it is thin and transparent.

Paint the centers of the flowers with Titanium White. Glaze Cadmium Yellow Medium Hue over the white on the bottom petals. Finally, add highlights by mixing Titanium White with the base color of the flowers. Go through and make any final adjustments, and the flowers are finished.

Lift the masking film from the planter box and paint in the same manner as the window frame. Use the 1/4-inch (6mm) filbert grass comb to create wood grain.

16 Add Final Touches

Remove the masking film from the final pansies and paint as before. Lightly glaze some Raw Sienna where the butterfly's wings meet the body. Rim the wings with Titanium White. Detail the butterfly's wings and body with Payne's Gray. You can add highlights to the body with Titanium White, if desired. Let dry, then glaze the wings with Dioxazine Purple.

waiting at the gate

I photographed this lovely Border Collie on my last trip to England, and for this painting, I placed him in a lush, cottage-garden setting. This project gives you an opportunity to paint loose foliage in the background, and to practice the stone and wood techniques shown on page 35.

Color Palette: Golden Fluid Acrylics

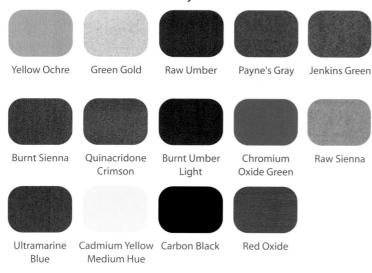

Yellow Ochre	Green Gold	Raw Umber	Payne's Gray	Jenkins Green
Burnt Sienna	Quinacridone Crimson	Burnt Umber Light	Chromium Oxide Green	Raw Sienna
Ultramarine Blue	Cadmium Yellow Medium Hue	Carbon Black	Red Oxide	

Liquitex Acrylic Artist Colors

Sap Green Permanent	Titanium White

Brushes: Silver
- Ultra Mini 2431S Designer Rounds nos. 12 and 6
- Ruby Satin 2528S Filbert Grass Comb 1/8-inch (3mm)
- Golden Natural Flat 2008S 3/4-inch (19mm)
- Cole Scruffy 2101S no. 2 flat

Other Supplies:
- 11" x 14" (28cm x 36cm) or larger Strathmore 500 series bristol board
- foamcore board
- white transfer paper
- wet palette
- sea sponge
- sharp craft knife
- masking film
- sharp pencil
- drafting tape
- Golden White Absorbent Ground

Prepare for Painting

Prepare the surface for painting by taping the bristol board securely to the foamcore support. Basecoat the entire paper with Burnt Umber Light. Enlarge the pattern at 106%. Trace and transfer the pattern to the basecoated paper. You do not need to transfer every detail of the foliage; we'll be painting a lot of that freehand. Apply the masking film and cut away the excess so only the dog and fence are covered.

1 Paint the Background

Sponge-paint the background foliage, beginning with Jenkins Green, then adding Green Gold and Raw Sienna. It should be lighter in the center and darker at the edges.

2 Add Leaf Shapes and the Fence

Paint loose, opaque leaf shapes in the background, using the no. 12 round brush and Sap Green Permanent, Yellow Ochre, Green Gold and Jenkins Green. Let dry, then remove the masking film from the gate and fence. Basecoat the fence with a mix of Ultramarine Blue and Titanium White. The paint doesn't need to be completely opaque; having the background colors peep through helps it look like painted wood.

3 Paint the Flagstones

Next paint the flagstones with a Raw Umber/Titanium White mix on a no. 12 round. If you lose track of the lines between the stones, you can transfer them again when the paint is dry. Add some Payne's Gray and Raw Umber glazes as the stones recede, so they blend into the background past the gate. You can also blend in some Jenkins Green, so the flagstones and foliage merge.

4 Add Texture to the Flagstones

Lightly sponge a texture onto the flagstones with Raw Umber. (You may use crumpled platic wrap instead, if you wish.) Mix a warm gray with Raw Umber, Titanium White and a touch of Payne's Gray, and paint an opaque layer, using the sponged texture as a guide. Make several shades of gray and scumble them into the stone, using the scruffy brush. The photo shows the flagstones in various stages.

5 Detail the Stones

Switch to the no. 12 round brush, and detail the stones by adding a few darks and lights and emphasizing some of the texture. Glaze a little Chromium Oxide Green along some of the edges. Add shadows under the dog and along the floral border. Make sure the stones have less detail and contrast as they recede. Finish with a little moss peeking between the stones, painted with Chromium Oxide Green and detailed with Jenkins Green and a little Titanium White.

6 Work on the Fence and Gate

Before working on the fence and gate, first slip-slap on some Sap Green Permanent where the floral border will go to establish color and placement. Next, add form to the wooden fence by glazing with Payne's Gray mixed with a touch of Raw Umber. You can add a few additional glazes of Raw Sienna, if desired.

7 Finish the Fence

Finish the fence by painting wood grain, using the 1/8-inch (3mm) filbert grass comb. Begin with Payne's Gray, then add lighter streaks with a Titanium White/Ultramarine Blue mix. Glaze a little Ultramarine Blue over the top if the fence starts looking too gray and dull. You can also add a few more glazes of Raw Sienna for warmth.

8 Paint the Leaves

Using Burnt Umber Light, indicate some twigs and branches overlapping the fence. Freehand-paint some leaves with White Absorbent Ground. If you decide to use Titanium White rather than absorbent ground, use the Liquitex brand rather than the Golden, as the Liquitex is less glossy. When the white leaves are dry, paint them with a mix of Cadmium Yellow Medium Hue and Yellow Ochre. In the photo, the leaves on the left are absorbent ground only, while the leaves on the right have been painted with the yellow mix.

9 Detail the Leaves and Basecoat the Dog

Begin adding details to the leaves by painting the center veins with Jenkins Green, using the no. 6 round brush. Now add form and detail, using Raw Sienna, Sap Green Permanent, and a mix of Quinacridone Crimson and Red Oxide. Make sure the leaves in the front are brighter and more detailed than those in the rear. The photo shows this in progress. Switch to the no. 12 round brush and basecoat the dog as shown, using Carbon Black and Titanium White. The collar is Quinacridone Crimson.

10

11

12

10 Paint the Black-Eyed Susans

Slip-slap some more foliage into the borders, first with Jenkins Green, then add some deeper darks with a mix of Jenkins Green and Quinacridone Crimson. Mix Sap Green Permanent with Titanium White and paint the stems of the black-eyed Susans, then add leaves. Mix Cadmium Yellow Medium Hue with a little Titanium White, and paint the flowers on the stems. Add a Burnt Umber Light center. The flowers in the foreground should be larger.

11 Glaze the Flowers and Leaves

Glaze some Cadmium Yellow Medium Hue over the flowers, and add a touch of Red Oxide to the center while the paint is still wet. Let dry, then begin glazing Jenkins Green over the leaves and stems. Add a few Burnt Umber Light glazes here and there.

12 Add Detail to the Dog

Begin with the nose and mouth, using the no. 6 round brush. Mix gray from Titanium White and Carbon Black for the highlights on the nose and lip. Add white teeth and some dark gray hairs around the nose. Glaze a little Burnt Umber Light across the front of the nose. Outline around the eyes with Carbon Black. With a 1/8-inch (3mm) filbert grass comb, use the gray mix to paint fur strokes across the Carbon Black fur of the face. Go back with pure black and start building form. For the white fur, start with a mix of Titanium White with a touch of Raw Sienna. Create darks with a mix of Raw Umber and Titanium White. Finally, add strokes of pure Titanium White over the top. The photo shows the fur in several stages.

13 Continue Painting the Fur

Continue painting the fur of the head, and gradually move down the chest and back. Give the eyes a Carbon Black pupil, a Raw Sienna secondary highlight and a Titanium White primary highlight.

14 Finish Painting the Dog

Finish the legs and tail. Paint the two legs that are overlapped by fur first. Use Burnt Umber Light to add warmth between the toes and on the tummy. Pay close attention to where you place the lights in the black fur. That's how you indicate the roundness of the animal's form underneath. As dark as the fur is, you don't want it to appear as a solid mass. Make sure that you paint in the direction of fur growth as well, so that your strokes taper toward the ends. I painted all the body fur with the 1/8-inch (3mm) filbert grass comb, with the exception of the feet, which I detailed with the no. 6 round brush. Check to see if the background behind the dog is so dark so that the black fur blends in too much. If this is the case, lighten the background behind his head with glazes of Green Gold mixed with a touch of Titanium White.

wren & blackberries

In this, our first watercolor demo, I used complementary colors to draw attention to the focal point of the wren. Red and green are complements, so I contrasted the warm reddish brown feathers against the green background. I used a blue shade of red for the berries so they didn't compete with the bird for attention. The area of white around the eye is the place of highest contrast between light and dark, so that is ultimately where the viewer's eye rests.

Color Palette: Winsor & Newton Watercolors

Olive Green	Hooker's Green	French Ultramarine	Brown Madder	Winsor Yellow	Permanent Sap Green
Burnt Umber	Burnt Sienna	Alizarin Crimson	Raw Sienna	Payne's Gray	Titanium White

Brushes: Silver
- Ultra Mini 2431S Designer Rounds nos. 12, 6 and 2
- Black Velvet Oval 3009S 3/4-inch (19mm)

Other Supplies:
- 9" x 12" (23cm x 30cm) Canson Montval watercolor paper block
- palette
- water container
- graphite transfer paper
- sharp pencil
- kneaded eraser
- sharp craft knife
- masking film
- drafting tape

Prepare for Painting

Reduce the pattern at 93%. Trace and transfer the pattern, and use a kneaded eraser to soften any lines that are too dark. I like to use drafting tape to mask off the edges of the painting so they stay tidy. Apply the masking film and smooth out any bubbles. Using your sharp craft knife (remember to use a new blade for each painting), cut out the outline of the entire design, then peel away to expose the background.

1 Paint the Background

Wet the background with clean water. Using the Black Velvet Oval brush, paint the entire background with a mix of Olive Green and Hooker's Green. While it is still wet, make vague leaf shapes with a mix of Brown Madder and Hooker's Green. For the darkest touches, add a little French Ultramarine to the mix. Let dry.

2 Develop the Background

Switch to the no. 6 round brush and paint twiggy little branches in the background, using Brown Madder with only a touch of Hooker's Green. Add some berry stems with the same mix, a little darker. Switch to the no. 12 brush, add more Hooker's Green and paint a few leaf shapes. Finally, paint some lighter leaf shapes with the Olive Green/Hooker's Green mix. This all helps to add texture to the background and a little depth to your painting.

3 Paint the Midground Berries

Remove the masking film from the areas in the drawing that are behind other elements. This exposes the middle ground of the painting. Basecoat the elements as shown using the no. 12 round brush. Paint the leaves one at a time with Permanent Sap Green, and drop in some Winsor Yellow while the green is still wet. Also sparingly add a few touches of Brown Madder here and there to the leaves. Make sure each leaf is dry before you paint the one touching it. For the berries, basecoat some with Payne's Gray and some with Alizarin Crimson, as shown. The berry calyxes are very pale (watery) Brown Madder.

4 Shade the Leaves and Berries

To add form, begin by shading the leaves, using a mix of Permanent Sap Green/French Ultramarine. Pick which side of the leaves is receiving less light, and paint shadows on those sides from the center vein outwards.

Next add a little shadow where the leaves overlap, and a little details to the veins. I've let the yellow bleeding into the green to become part of the leaf texture.

For the berries, shade one side of the blackberries with Payne's Gray. Try lifting out lighter areas on the leaves and berries with clean water on your brush. The stems and red berries are shaded with a mix of Alizarin Crimson and Hooker's Green. Mixing a color with a little bit of its complement is a good way to create a shadow tone. I used the no. 12 round brush for this step, but you may feel more comfortable with the no. 6.

5 Add Details to the Leaves and Berries

With the no. 6 round brush, add more details to the leaves with some of the shading mixture. Blend with a clean, damp brush.

For the berries, outline each little segment, using Payne's Gray for the blackberries and the Alizarin Crimson shadow mix for the red berries. Continue defining the stems, including adding thorns, with Brown Madder.

Now remove the masking film from the next group of midground leaves. Leave the masking film on the objects that overlap, such as berries or other leaves. If any paint has seeped under the masking film, lift it by going over it with clean water, then blotting with a tissue.

Watercolor Blocks

A watercolor block is a pad of paper gummed on all four sides, which eliminates the risk of paper buckling. When you are finished painting, release the top sheet of paper by running a butter knife around all the edges. If you prefer to work with an individual sheet of paper rather than a block, tape it on all four sides to a sturdy support, such as foamcore board (see "Mounting the Paper to Prevent Buckling" on page 8).

6 Paint Midground Leaves

Paint the exposed leaves as before. The photo shows the leaves with the basecoat and the shadow side indicated.

7 Continue Painting Leaves

Keep removing masking film and painting leaves as they overlap, until all the leaves are painted. Add a few holes in the leaves, rimmed with Brown Madder, for a natural look. Remove the masking film from the butterfly and the wren. The foreground berries should be the only things still covered.

8 Basecoat the Wren and Butterfly

Using the no. 12 round brush, paint the wren with a wash of Raw Sienna, leaving the white areas as white paper. Give the butterfly a wash of French Ultramarine, leaving the edges of the wings white. The wren's eye and leg are Burnt Umber.

9 Add Brown to the Wren

Lay in the brown areas on the wren with a mix of Burnt Umber/Burnt Sienna. For the darkest browns, including the beak, add a little Payne's Gray to the mix. Paint the butterfly's body with Payne's Gray. Notice how the reddish brown of the wren stands out from the complementary green background.

10 Detail the Wren

To detail the wren, use the no. 2 round brush. Begin with the eye: a Payne's Gray pupil and Titanium White highlight. Next, using the Payne's Gray/Burnt Umber mix, build form on the wren's face and breast. It is very easy when painting a bird's face to make it look angry. Emphasizing the darks behind the eye and downplaying the darks in front of and on top of the eye will usually alleviate this. Use Titanium White to pull out a few feathers on the chin, on top of the head and under the tail.

11 Build the Wren's Form

Start building form on the wing, back, belly and tail, using Burnt Umber and either the no. 6 or no. 2 round brush. Add shading to the leg and the darks of the wing with the Burnt Umber/Payne's Gray mix. You can add more Raw Sienna washes to the breast if it seems pale. Add a little shading to the butterfly's wings with a French Ultramarine/Alizarin Crimson mix. Tone down the white wing edges slightly with a very thin glaze of Payne's Gray.

12 Add Highlights to the Wren

Add highlights to the wren's wing, back and tail by lifting them out with the no. 6 brush dampened with clean water. It should be moist, but not dripping. (See "Lifting Out Color" on page 14.) For the breast, mix Titanium White and Raw Sienna.

13 Paint the Foreground Berries

Remove the remaining masking film and paint the foreground berries as before. Detail the calyx leaves with a mix of Brown Madder and Permanent Sap Green.

14 Finish the Butterfly

Glaze a very thin wash of Burnt Umber across the butterfly's wings and let dry. Detail the body with Payne's Gray, and add Titanium White highlights. Add a thin rim to the wings with a Payne's Gray/Burnt Umber mix, and use the same mix where the wings meet the body. Add faint dots to the wings with transparent Payne's Gray. Using a sharp pencil, add antennae and delicate little wing veins.

15 Finish the Blackberries

Shade each little segment with the same mix used for outlining it. Add a few highlights with Titanium White, but not to every segment because some are in the shade. Create a few leaf highlights by lifting them out with a clean, damp brush, as you did on the wren.

tulip twins

In this painting of cute twin bunnies, we'll use a technique that is impossible with acrylics: lifting color from a dry background with a clean, damp brush. To create this painting with acrylics, you will need to add some opaque layers.

Color Palette: Winsor & Newton Watercolors

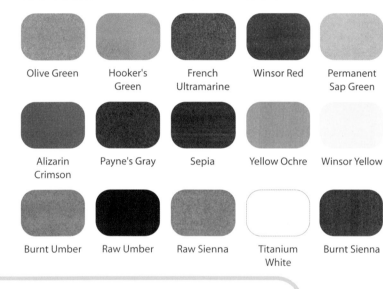

Olive Green · Hooker's Green · French Ultramarine · Winsor Red · Permanent Sap Green

Alizarin Crimson · Payne's Gray · Sepia · Yellow Ochre · Winsor Yellow

Burnt Umber · Raw Umber · Raw Sienna · Titanium White · Burnt Sienna

Brushes: Silver
- Ultra Mini 2431S Designer Rounds nos. 12, 6 and 2
- Golden Natural Flat 2008S 3/4-inch (19mm)
- Black Velvet Oval 3009S 3/4-inch (19mm)
- Ruby Satin 2528S Filbert Grass comb 1/8-inch (3mm)

Other Supplies:
- 9" x 12" (23cm x 30cm) Canson Montval watercolor paper block
- palette
- water container
- graphite transfer paper
- sharp pencil
- kneaded eraser
- sharp craft knife
- masking film
- drafting tape
- red pastel pencil
- cotton swab

Prepare for Painting

Enlarge the pattern at 118%. Trace and transfer the pattern. I use drafting tape to mask off the edges of the paper so they stay tidy. Apply the masking film as usual, and cut around the drawing to expose the background. It is important not to cut too deeply, as you don't want to score the paper beneath. Pay close attention when you remove the masking film from between the tulips, as it is easy to get confused between what is leaf and what is grass.

1 Paint the Background

Wet the entire background with clean water, then paint with Winsor Yellow, using the 3/4-inch (19mm) flat brush. Let dry. Wet the surface again. Using the 3/4-inch (19mm) oval brush, paint loose green shapes across the background, beginning with Olive Green. Olive green is a good example of a sedimentary color—you will see that it dries looking a little grainy. I like the texture this can add to a nature painting. Add a little French Ultramarine to the top right side. Finally, mix Hooker's Green with Payne's Gray and make loose foliage shapes. Make sure the surface is not too wet or it will puddle against the masking film. If this happens, gently soak up some of the water by dipping the corner of a tissue into it. Let dry completely.

2 Add Grass to the Background

First, lift out some lighter blades of grass with clean water and a no. 6 round brush. Next, add darker details with the Hooker's Green/Payne's Gray mix. Finally, add some Yellow Ochre to the tips and edges of some of the blades.

Tip

Lifting out color is a great way to achieve light areas without using white. Make sure the paint is completely dry before lifting out the color. For more on this technique, see page 14.

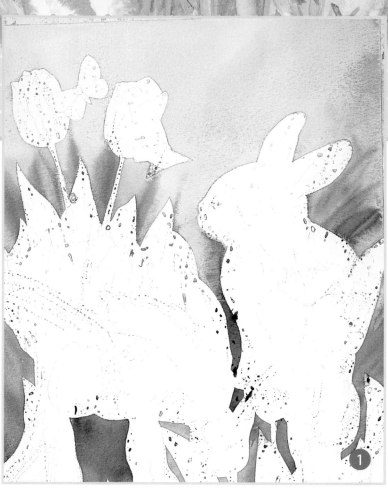

3 Basecoat the Tulip Leaves

Now remove the masking film from the tulip leaves that are overlapped by other leaves or stems. Basecoat the leaves with Permanent Sap Green. Add a little Raw Sienna to the tips of some of the leaves while they are still wet. Create the darks with a mix of French Ultramarine and Permanent Sap Green once the basecoat is dry. Finally, deepen some areas with a glaze of Alizarin Crimson.

4 Paint the Background Tulips

When the leaves are dry, lift the masking film from the background tulips. Paint the stems with Permanent Sap Green, and add Alizarin Crimson shadows. For the flowers, work one petal at a time, and allow each petal to dry before painting the one touching it. Begin by painting the entire petal with a wash of Winsor Yellow. While the yellow is still wet, add some Alizarin Crimson at the top of the petal and a touch of Hooker's Green at the bottom. Finally, paint the remaining leaves behind the left-hand bunny, and add a little shading with Raw Umber.

5 Basecoat the Bunnies

Using the no. 12 round brush, basecoat the bunnies with Raw Umber. Notice how I have left some areas of white paper showing, and in other areas I have lifted out the lights with a clean, damp brush. The eye is Burnt Umber, and the insides of the ears are a mix of Alizarin Crimson and Yellow Ochre.

6 Add Detail to the Eyes and Fur

Paint the pupil of the eye and the other bunny's closed eyes with a black mixed from Burnt Umber/Payne's Gray. Add details around the eye with Sepia. Paint a dot of Titanium White for a highlight, and wipe out the secondary highlight with clean water. Use clean water on the 1/8-inch (3mm) filbert grass comb to soften the edges of the bunny's chest and back. Finally, add a few white hairs on the chest. Notice how I also added some Raw Umber to the grass by the right-hand bunny, as if a little bit of his body was peeping through the blades.

7 Continue Painting the Fur

Glaze some Burnt Umber over the bunnies as shown. Add a wash of Sepia inside the ears. Let dry, then begin painting fur, using Sepia and the 1/8-inch (3mm) filbert grass comb. Use Raw Umber for the fur on the white part of the chest. The head has strokes of both Burnt Umber and Sepia. If the fur looks too rough, soften it with clean water on the no. 12 round brush. The photo shows the left bunny with the wash only and the right bunny with fur strokes added.

8 Add a Few White Hairs

Now, some people are purists when it comes to watercolor, and don't approve of using white paint, so if you wish, it is fine to stop working on the fur at this point. You can scratch out a few white hairs with the tip of your craft knife, if desired. I like to add a few light hairs with Titanium White mixed with a little Yellow Ochre. Let dry, then glaze a little transparent Raw Sienna over the top. Add a little Burnt Sienna for the darker areas.

9 Add Details to the Painting

Bring some blades of grass up over the bottom of the sleepy bunny. First, lift them out with a clean, damp brush, then paint with Hooker's Green. Draw in a few whiskers with a sharp pencil, and add a few delicate white hairs around the eye and ears. If you wish, you can accentuate the inside of the ears by a rubbing a cotton swab across a red pastel pencil. Then use the pigment on the swab to paint a soft blush of color.

Tip

White paint can look cold and gray, especially when applied over a brown, so I like to warm it up by adding a little Yellow Ochre or a similar warm color to it. Also, when using white, make sure to pick Titanium White over Zinc White if you want it to be opaque.

10 Paint the Foreground Tulips

Paint the remaining tulips as you did the background tulips in Steps 3 and 4. These tulips are in the foreground, so pay a little extra attention to detail. Try adding a glaze of Winsor Yellow to help bring them forward. The only things that still should be covered by masking film are the butterflies.

11 Paint the Butterflies

Remove the masking film from the butterflies and paint their bodies with Sepia, using a no. 6 round brush. Next, mix an orange from Winsor Yellow with the addition of a small amount of Winsor Red. Paint the orange areas on the wings, and blend with clean water. Let dry, then detail with more Sepia on a no. 2 brush as shown. Finally draw the wing veins and the antennae with a sharp pencil.

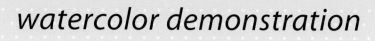

watercolor demonstration

tea for three

This design of a mother sparrow and her three babies is quite busy, but don't be intimidated. Each element is handled one at a time, which will help keep you from being overwhelmed. This is an example of why I prefer masking film to masking fluid, because you could never remove the fluid from one small area at a time as you can when using the film.

Color Palette: Winsor & Newton Watercolors

Olive Green	Hooker's Green	Payne's Gray	Permanent Rose	French Ultramarine	Titanium White
Raw Sienna	Winsor Blue (green shade)	Permanent Sap Green	Winsor Violet	Winsor Yellow	
Burnt Sienna	Burnt Umber	Sepia	Yellow Ochre	Raw Umber	

Brushes: Silver
- Ultra Mini 2431S Designer Rounds nos. 12, 6 and 2
- Golden Natural Flat 2008S 3/4-inch (19mm)
- Ruby Satin 2528S Filbert Grass Comb 1/8-inch (3mm)

Other Supplies:
- 9" x 12" (23cm x 30cm) or larger Canson Montval watercolor block
- drafting tape
- masking film
- sharp pencil
- water container
- transfer paper
- palette
- small spritzer bottle

Prepare for Painting

Enlarge the pattern at 133%. Trace and transfer the pattern. Use drafting tape to mask off the painting's borders to keep them tidy. Next, apply the masking film and carefully cut away to expose the background. This will require some concentration, as there are lots of little nooks and crannies between the flowers and leaves.

1 Paint the Background

Wet the entire background with clean water using the 3/4-inch (19mm) flat brush. While the paper is still wet, paint a wash of Olive Green over the entire background with the same brush. Working quickly, before it dries, introduce some Hooker's Green along the sides and bottom, making vague, grasslike shapes. Finally, mix some Payne's Gray with Hooker's Green and paint this darker green around the bottom third of the picture. When you work this wet, there may be some seepage under the masking film, but it is nothing to worry about. The paint can easily be lifted with clean water on your brush when you are ready to paint that area.

2 Paint the Soft-Focus Flowers

Using the spritzer bottle, spray a few damp patches on the background. Gently drop in a little Permanent Rose or French Ultramarine to the center of each wet patch, and let the color bleed out to the edges. This will give the effect of out-of-focus flower blossoms.

3 Paint the Grass

Use more of the dark green mixed from the Hooker's Green and Payne's Gray. With the edge of the 3/4-inch (19mm) flat brush, paint strokes of grass. Let dry, then paint more strokes with Raw Sienna. Finally, add more Payne's Gray to the green mix and paint some deeper darks.

4 Basecoat the Chicory Flowers

Remove the masking film from the blue chicory flowers and stems in the background. Don't forget the leaves by the mama bird's tail. If you have any areas where the paint has seeped under the masking film, lift it by wiping it with a clean, damp brush (don't scrub!), and blotting with a tissue. Basecoat the flowers with thin French Ultramarine and the stems and leaves with Permanent Sap Green, using the no. 6 round brush.

5 Detail the Flower Petals

With the no. 6 round brush, begin detailing the flower petals with French Ultramarine, and add a few glazes of Winsor Blue to a few of them. Paint a little Titanium White in the center of each flower. Let dry, then add stamens with a mix of Payne's Gray and French Ultramarine, and give each a white tip. You can add shadows with glazes of the same mix, but use it sparingly.

6 Paint More Flowers

Mix a little Permanent Rose with Hooker's Green and use it to paint the center vein and shadow side of the chicory leaf. Let dry, then add details with the same mix. Detail the stems as well. Next, remove the masking film from the background clover. Basecoat the flowers with Permanent Rose, and for the leaves and stems, mix a light, yellowy green from Winsor Blue and Winsor Yellow. Make sure each element is dry before you paint the one touching it.

7 Detail the Clover Blossoms

Paint a few strokes of Permanent Sap Green up the center of the clover blossom. Mix Titanium White with Permanent Rose and paint pale pink petals. Finally, add dark details with Permanent Rose mixed with just a touch of Hooker's Green. The photo shows this in stages. Finally, use Permanent Sap Green to paint leaf details.

8 Detail the Clover Leaves

Continue using the no. 6 round brush to paint shadow areas on the clover leaves with very thin and transparent French Ultramarine. Rim the edges of the leaves behind the primroses with Permanent Rose. Detail the leaves with Hooker's Green. Remove the masking film from the background primroses.

9 Begin the Primroses

Basecoat each primrose leaf with Olive Green, and drop in some Permanent Sap Green while the Olive Green is still wet. The flower stems are a mix of Permanent Sap Green and Olive Green. Next, paint the primrose center with Winsor Yellow. Make sure it is thoroughly dry, then paint the petals with Winsor Violet. Draw a circle with Burnt Umber in the middle of the yellow center.

10 Add Detail to the Stem and Leaves

Still using the no. 6 round brush, now moistened with clean water, lift out the center vein on the leaves. Let dry, then begin detailing, using Hooker's Green mixed with a touch of Permanent Rose. The photo shows this in progress. Detail the yellow part of the flowers with Raw Sienna, and use Winsor Violet mixed with a touch of French Ultramarine on the petals. Once the shading on the leaves is dry, add highlights with touches of Winsor Yellow and Titanium White. Finally, glaze some Permanent Rose on the flower stems.

11 Basecoat the Baby Birds

Now remove the masking film from the baby sparrows in the nest. Paint a little bit of Sepia behind the left-hand sparrow to show how the nest wraps around it. Let dry, then basecoat the babies with very light Raw Umber. The breasts should be lighter than their heads; you can lift the color with a damp brush if it gets too dark. The beaks are Winsor Yellow, and the eyes are Burnt Umber.

12 Detail the Feathers and Features

Mix an orange from Permanent Rose and Raw Sienna and paint the inside of the open beak. The darks are added with Sepia. Detail the eyes with a Payne's Gray pupil and Titanium White highlight. Add a light ring around the eyes with Sepia. Switch to the 1/8-inch (3mm) filbert grass comb and paint loose feather strokes. Remember that baby chicks have downy feathers, so don't try to make them look too smooth. Next, add some Burnt Umber strokes, then refine the feathers a bit with the no. 2 round brush. Add a few Raw Sienna strokes to the breast (you can also add a few Titanium White strokes if desired).

13 Finish the Baby Birds

Finish the chicks by detailing their beaks. Using the no. 2 round brush, paint Burnt Sienna at the tip, then put in the darks with thin Sepia. Add Titanium White highlights if you wish. Now remove the masking film from the nest and from more of the primrose leaves, if they are behind flowers or other leaves. Basecoat the nest with Raw Sienna, and paint the primrose leaves as before. When the nest is dry, you can add a few overlapping twigs with a mix of Raw Sienna/Titanium White.

14 Begin Shading the Nest

Continue removing masking film from the midground leaves and flowers, and paint them as before. All the foreground foliage still should be covered. Begin shading the nest with Raw Umber. Finally, remove the masking film from the saucer, but not the cup. Paint the saucer shadows with a gray mixed from Sepia and French Ultramarine. Let dry, then glaze with Yellow Ochre. Leave the lightest areas as plain paper. Finally, paint a Permanent Sap Green stripe.

15 Finish the Nest

Now paint the flowers and leaves that overlap the saucer. Let's also finish the nest, so we can get ready to tackle the teacup! Use Sepia to draw the straw that makes the nest, then color some of the stems with Olive Green, Raw Umber or Yellow Ochre. Next, you can lift the masking film from the teacup, but leave the butterfly covered.

16 Paint the Teacup

Paint the teacup in the same manner as you painted the saucer. Notice the strip of reflected light on the left side of the cup by the handle. Also add a very faint wash of Permanent Sap Green to both sides of the cup to indicate that it is reflecting its green surroundings. Next, use the no. 6 round moistened with clean water to lift out blades of grass in the foreground. Bring some blades up over the saucer and some of the leaves. Tint some of them with Burnt Sienna, and darken between others with a Hooker's Green/French Ultramarine mix. You can add some Olive Green too, if you wish. Continue painting the primroses. The photo shows the grass in progress.

17 Basecoat the Mama Bird

Lift the masking film from the final clover and chicory and paint them as you did before. Next, uncover the mama bird. Give the mother sparrow a basecoat of Raw Umber, then add some Burnt Umber to the wings and Payne's Gray to the face, as shown. Leave the white areas as plain paper. The eye and leg are also Burnt Umber.

18 Detail the Cup and Bird

Next paint the pink design on the cup. Feel free to change the design if you wish, but keep it simple, as the surrounding foliage is rather detailed. Now, remove the masking film from the butterfly and paint the wings with French Ultramarine. The body is Payne's Gray. Let's move back to the mama bird while the butterfly dries. Add a patch of Winsor Yellow above the eye, and begin detailing with Payne's Gray and the no. 2 round brush, as shown.

19 Finish the Butterfly

Detail the butterfly's body with more Payne's Gray. Glaze a little Burnt Sienna where the wings meet the body. Rim the blue portion of the wings with a Payne's Gray/Burnt Sienna mix. Let dry, then add very faint Payne's Gray dots to the wings. Glaze a little Winsor Violet over the Burnt Sienna. Finally, add darker Payne's Gray details where the wings meet the body, and draw in antennae and wing veins with a sharp pencil.

20 Finish the Mama Bird

Switch to the no. 6 round brush and begin glazing with thin Sepia on the bird's back, tail, and where the breast meets the wing. Let dry, then add details with delicate Sepia strokes. Add a little Payne's Gray mixed with a touch of Titanium White to the top of the wing. You can use a no. 2 round for the details if you wish.

21 Add Final Touches

Finish the grass by pulling some blades up over the primrose leaves. (You can use Titanium White to make the grass blades more opaque, if necessary.) Add some highlights and a few opaque feathers to mother sparrow with Titanium White mixed with a little Yellow Ochre, then stand back and admire your work. This has been our most complicated painting, so you should feel proud of a job well done!

part three:
gallery
place your own pet in any painting

In this section you'll find even more adorable animals to paint on pages 120-123! The colors you'll need for each animal or bird are pointed out, so just use the painting techniques you've learned in the earlier demonstrations to try your hand at it.

But first, let me show you in three easy steps how to make your own beloved pet the star of any painting! In the example on these pages, I used the scene from "Good Buddies" (page 44) and placed a different cat and dog into the painting. You can do the same with photos of your own pets.

Here's a list of the supplies you'll need: several sheets of clear acetate, some vellum paper, a roll of tape, a fine-tip permanent ink pen (not a ballpoint), and a craft knife. You'll find these at any arts and crafts supply store. You may also need to use a photocopier to enlarge or reduce your pattern.

1 Trace a pattern on a sheet of vellum of the painting you want to use. (Vellum works better than tracing paper because it's a heavier weight paper, yet still transparent.) We will be replacing the dog and cat in this painting with a different dog and cat. Use a craft knife to carefully remove just the animals from the pattern.

2 Choose good, clear photographs of the pets you are going to use as replacements. Place each photo under a sheet of clear acetate and trace the pet onto the acetate using a fine tip permanent-ink pen. If the pet is seated or standing in the opposite direction you need, the clear acetate can be flipped over so the pet will be in the correct position. The cat pattern shown here will be flipped over so it fits better in the new painting. Enlarge the drawing using a photocopier so the new animal is the same size as the animal being replaced. After you find the right size of enlargement, photocopy the acetate drawing onto a sheet of vellum to use as a pattern.

3 Next, tape the "replacement" animals into the proper spots on the vellum of the original pattern. Now you have your "new" pattern. Transfer the pattern onto watercolor paper or bristol board and start to paint. Paint your pets the appropriate colors and follow the directions for "Good Buddies" on pages 44-51 to paint the rest of the picture.

You don't have to be a slave to your reference photos. Feel free to change things to make your painting work better. In this painting, I've curved the cat's tail inward, which helps lead the viewer's eyes around the painting. And I've added a colorful bandanna to the dog.

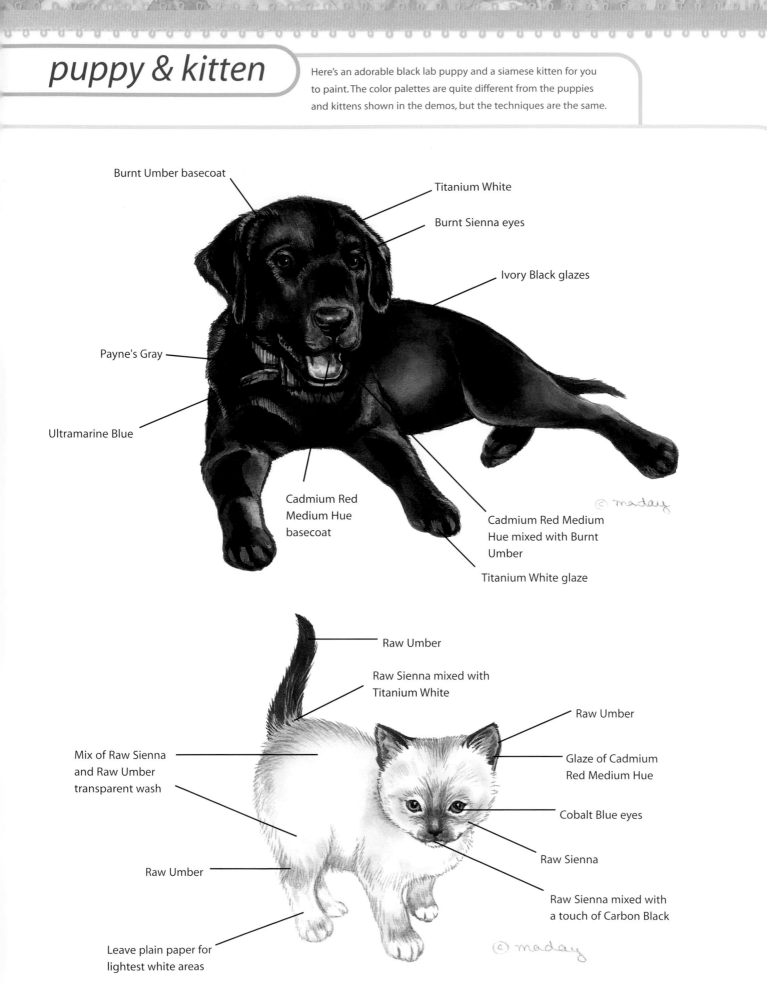

puppy & kitten

Here's an adorable black lab puppy and a siamese kitten for you to paint. The color palettes are quite different from the puppies and kittens shown in the demos, but the techniques are the same.

Burnt Umber basecoat

Titanium White

Burnt Sienna eyes

Ivory Black glazes

Payne's Gray

Ultramarine Blue

Cadmium Red Medium Hue basecoat

Cadmium Red Medium Hue mixed with Burnt Umber

Titanium White glaze

Raw Umber

Raw Sienna mixed with Titanium White

Raw Umber

Glaze of Cadmium Red Medium Hue

Cobalt Blue eyes

Mix of Raw Sienna and Raw Umber transparent wash

Raw Sienna

Raw Umber

Raw Sienna mixed with a touch of Carbon Black

Leave plain paper for lightest white areas

120

butterflies

Here I have painted several different types of butterflies and moths. You can use these as reference when creating your own designs.

Cadmium Yellow Medium Hue basecoat

Titanium White

Black colored-pencil details

Ultramarine Blue mixed with a little Titanium White

Carbon Black

Quinacridone Gold

Burnt Sienna

Black colored-pencil antennae

Cadmium Yellow Medium Hue basecoat

Raw Umber mixed with Carbon Black

Raw Umber

Burnt Sienna

Raw Umber mixed with Quinacridone Gold

Carbon Black

Quinacridone Gold

Yellow Ochre mixed with Titanium White

Titanium White

Raw Umber shading

Carbon Black with Titanium White details

Raw Umber

Burnt Sienna

Yellow Ochre basecoat

Quinacridone Gold

Raw Umber

Yellow Ochre glaze

Raw Umber with Carbon Black details

Yellow Ochre mixed with Titanium White basecoat

Use a sharp colored pencil for antennae and wing veins if you are unsteady with the brush.

chick & duckling

Chicks and ducklings have soft, downy feathers, which makes them different from adult birds. I think you will find using a grass comb brush to be invaluable in achieving a fluffy look.

Yellow Ochre basecoat

Glaze of Cadmium Yellow Medium Hue

Quinacridone Gold

Burnt Umber shading

Burnt Umber eye with Carbon Black pupil, Titanium White highlight

Quinacridone Gold

Titanium White mixed with Cadmium Yellow Medium Hue

Burnt Umber shading

Titanium White mixed with Cadmium Yellow Medium Hue

Quinacridone Gold with Burnt Umber shading

© maday

Raw Umber over Burnt Umber shading

Yellow Ochre basecoat

Quinacridone Gold

Payne's Gray glaze over Burnt Umber/Quinacridone Gold mix

Titanium White

Titanium White mixed with Cadmium Yellow Medium Hue

Glaze of Cadmium Yellow Medium Hue

Burnt Umber mixed with Quinacridone Gold

Titanium White

Payne's Gray

rooster

Roosters are popular subjects for painters because of the lovely, glossy sheen to their feathers. I used various sizes of round brushes, and lots of glazing to create vivid colors and smooth feathers.

Basecoat the entire rooster except the tail with Quinacridone Gold.

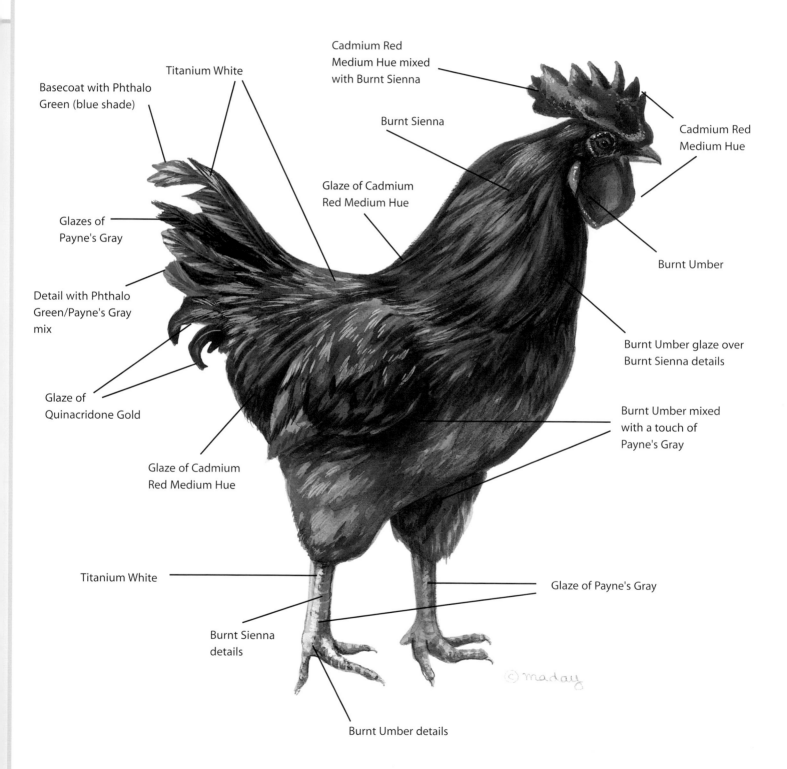

Titanium White

Basecoat with Phthalo Green (blue shade)

Cadmium Red Medium Hue mixed with Burnt Sienna

Burnt Sienna

Cadmium Red Medium Hue

Glaze of Cadmium Red Medium Hue

Glazes of Payne's Gray

Burnt Umber

Detail with Phthalo Green/Payne's Gray mix

Burnt Umber glaze over Burnt Sienna details

Glaze of Quinacridone Gold

Burnt Umber mixed with a touch of Payne's Gray

Glaze of Cadmium Red Medium Hue

Titanium White

Glaze of Payne's Gray

Burnt Sienna details

Burnt Umber details

mini demo patterns

Wren, page 20

White cat, page 24

Baby Bird, page 19

Lamb, page 21

Fawn, page 22

Bunny, page 23

Flowers, page 34

Beagle Puppy, page 26

Berries, page 32

Ginger-Striped Kitten, page 30

White Terrier, page 28

resources

My thanks go to the manufacturers who assisted me with products and information: Dee Silver at Silver Brush Ltd., Mark Golden at Golden Artist Colors, David Pyle at Winsor & Newton, and Canson, Inc.

Author: Jane Maday
E-mail: Jmaday1@msn.com

Paints, Brushes & Paper

Golden Artist Colors, Inc.
188 Bell Road
New Berlin, NY 13411-9527
www.goldenpaints.com

Silver Brush Ltd.
P.O. Box 414
Windsor, NJ 08561-0414
www.silverbrush.com

Winsor & Newton
P.O. Box 1396
Piscataway, NJ 08855
www.winsornewton.com

Canson, Inc.
21 Industrial Drive
South Hadley, MA 01075
www.canson-us.com

Canadian Retailers

Crafts Canada
120 North Archibald St.
Thunder Bay, ON P7C 3X8
888-482-5978
www.craftscanada.ca

Folk Art Enterprises
P.O. Box 1088
Ridgetown, ON, N0P 2C0
Tel: 800-265-9434

MacPherson Arts & Crafts
91 Queen St. E.
P.O. Box 1810
St. Mary's, ON, N4X 1C2
Tel: 800-238-6663
www.macphersoncrafts.com

Maureen McNaughton Enterprises
RR #2
Belwood, ON, N0B 1J0
Tel: 519-843-5648
www.maureenmcnaughton.com

U.K. Retailers

Atlantis Art Materials
7-9 Plumber's Row
London E1 1EQ
020 7377 8855
www.atlantisart.co.uk

Crafts World (head office)
No. 8 North Street
Guildford
Surrey GU1 4 AF
07000 757070

Green & Stone
259 Kings Road
London SW3 5EL
020 7352 0837
www.greenandstone.com

Help Desk
HobbyCraft Superstore
The Peel Centre
St. Ann Way
Gloucester
Gloucestershire GL1 5SF
01452 424999
www.hobbycraft.co.uk

index

the best in art instruction
is from North Light Books!

Lush & Lively Flowers You Can Paint

Paint the most realistic-looking flowers, leaves and foliage imaginable with Sharon Hamilton's two-stage approach. Sharon shows you how to build form and dimension with acrylics, using undercoats and intense dark and light colors, followed by oil paint to enhance the richness of the design. Whether you're a beginner or an experienced painter, you'll benefit from this book's easy instructional chapters and thoroughly enjoy painting the 10 gorgeous floral projects.

ISBN-13: 978-1-58180-443-0, paperback, 128 pages, #32691
ISBN-10: 1-58180-443-1, paperback, 128 pages, #32691

Painting Garden Animals with Sherry C. Nelson

Learn Sherry C. Nelson's innovative and creative techniques for painting all of your favorite garden animals. Through 10 step-by-step exercises, Nelson will guide you to master each part of the animal, including its eyes, nose, ears and paws, as well as painting realistic fur with distinctive color, markings and length.

ISBN-13: 978-1-58180-427-0, paperback, 144 pages, #32591
ISBN-10: 1-58180-427-X, paperback, 144 pages, #32591

Painting Animal Friends

With *Painting Animal Friends*, it's possible to paint cats, dogs, horses, or even ducks without any fine art training at all! There are over 27 different demonstrations of the most popular animals, each with a template line drawing to help get you started right away.

ISBN-13: 978-1-58180-598-7, paperback, 128 pages, #33111
ISBN-10: 1-58180-598-5, paperback, 128 pages, #33111

Painter's Quick Reference: Flowers & Blooms

This easy-to-use reference book provides inspiration and all the details you need to make your flower paintings come alive! With more than 50 popular garden flowers, wildflowers and even exotics, you'll find plenty of quick ideas for any painting project.

ISBN-13: 978-1-58180-761-5, paperback, 128 pages, #33430
ISBN-10: 1-58180-761-9, paperback, 128 pages, #33430

These books and other fine North Light titles are available at your local arts & crafts retailer, bookstore, or from on-line suppliers.